C000293789

The Power of...

SPICES

The Power of...
SPICES

Origins • Traditions • Facts and Flavours

Gill Davies

WORTH
WPRESS

First published in 2015
by Worth Press Ltd, Cambridge, England.
info@worthpress.co.uk

© Worth Press Ltd, 2015

Text © Gill Davies
The author has asserted her rights under the Copyright, Designs and Patents Act 1988
to be identified as the author of this work.

British Library Cataloguing in Publication Data. A catalogue record for this book is
available from the British Library

ISBN: 978-1-84931-092-5

10 9 8 7 6 5 4 3 2 1

Publisher's Note: While every effort has been made to ensure that the information
herein is complete and accurate, the publishers and author make no representations
or warranties either expressed or implied of any kind with respect to this book to the
reader. Neither the author nor the publishers shall be liable or responsible for any
damage, loss or expense of any kind arising out of information contained in this book.
The thoughts or opinions expressed in this book represent the personal views of the
author and not necessarily those of the publishers. Further, the publisher takes no
responsibility for third party websites or their content.

The publishers wish to record their thanks to Michael Starke of Essbro
for the guidance and help given in the preparation of this book

The images used in this book come from either the public domain or from the public
commons unless otherwise stated.

Design and layout: Arati Devasher, www.aratidevasher.com
Editor: Meredith MacArdle
Picture research: Meredith MacArdle, Arati Devasher

Printed and bound in China

CONTENTS

Introduction   8

Discovering the Spices   **15**
Seeds   17
Fruits and Berries   53
Bark, Trees and Resin   81
Roots, Bulbs and Rhizomes   97
Other Sources   117

Mixed Spices   139
The Story of Salt   147
The Spice Trade   155
Fascinating Facts   163
International Spices (Maps)   177
Sense and Emotion: 185
  The Meaning of Spices
Index   190
Image Credits   191
Author's Note, Acknowledgements   192
  and Bibliography

IRRITANTS, ALLERGENS AND TOXINS

Look out for this sign, indicating that certain parts of these plants are potentially harmful; they may be poisonous, induce allergic reactions or irritate skin and eyes.

KEY TO SYMBOLS

 MORE FOOD FACTS
 TRADITIONALLY USED FOR
 POISONS AND TOXINS

 MEDICINAL USE
 DID YOU KNOW?
 OTHER USES

INTRODUCTION

In *culinary* use, only the leafy green parts of any plant are classed as herbal; all its other elements (roots, seeds, berries, buds, resin or bark) serve as spices for flavouring, colouring or preserving food. Usually dried, spices are also sometimes used for medicinal, ritual and religious purposes or for making cosmetics and perfume. Some plants (like peppermint, parsley and bay) appear in both herb and spice listings, especially if different parts of the same plant are used or sometimes simply because the flavour is considered very spicy. Other plant parts, such as sesame and sunflower seeds, coconut flesh, and citrus fruit peels and zest, although not necessarily hot or pungent, also count as spices. And what an amazing range of fragrant, aromatic plant products present themselves under this category – a dazzling array of reds, golds, burnished browns, soft greens, russets, luscious purple and crackling white. All flaunt exciting possibilities … whether growing in their many natural settings, in pots and jars on supermarket and kitchen shelves, blazing in bulging sacksful in Oriental markets or in the pages of history books as we discover how spices drove trade, discovery and warfare.

Many of these scintillating flavourings (like cinnamon, cloves, ginger or pepper) are found in tropical and subtropical regions of the world. The very name 'spice' suggests hot, far-flung places –

Spices can come from roots, nuts, seeds, fruit, leaves or bark. Facing page: Spices come in a dazzling array of colours.

exotic lands warmed by equatorial sunshine as bright as mustard. Indeed, we use the term to 'spice up' our lives when an extra exciting element is introduced … just as a small pinch of nutmeg or a sprinkle of poppy seeds will add interest and texture to our food. And there are sweet spices too, like vanilla, peppermint and liquorice. A few spices do come from cooler climes but most have luxuriated in the warmth of places like the Pacific Islands, the Caribbean, Africa, or the Mediterranean coasts; some absorbing all the mysteries of Arabia, the magic of Persia or the fascination of the Far East.

As well as their role in our cooking adventures, these pungent, aromatic spices may also be used to preserve foods, make or enhance wines and spirits, create perfumes and cosmetics, conjure traditional medicines, make magic spells and embalm the dead. In ancient times some had strong associations with the gods – medieval spice lists include sandalwood and myrrh (which *can* be ingested by mixing with wine) but which are chiefly linked to religious ceremony. Myrrh, of course, was one of the three gifts presented by the Wise Men to the infant Jesus. So a spice does not have to be only for culinary use, and even if it is a foodstuff, it may have many other uses. For example, flax is used to make linen and musical instruments; the most expensive of spices, saffron, might be sprinkled over royal guests; ginseng is both sacred and an aphrodisiac. Garlic is said to ward off vampires, werewolves, witches and demons (and moles from your garden).

Sweet spices used for seasonal cooking.

Wearing bags of spice might ward off pestilence ... and, in fact, nutmeg could well have repelled the plague-carrying fleas – whether it did or not, European spice traders sold it at a profit of almost six thousand per cent.

From its beginnings in the Middle East over 4,000 years ago, the Spice Trade developed and flourished. As enterprises became more lucrative, trade in the aromatic pungent spices – and control of the places where they thrived – emerged as major wellsprings of wealth and power. Spice locations were often kept secret and the routes to reach them (whether shipping lanes or long, overland spice routes) were fraught with

Spices have been a part of religion for millennia.

danger and piracy; the Spice Trade was both highly remunerative and extremely perilous. Sources were tightly controlled, guarded and fought over. Spices made merchants immensely rich, gave

Frankincense and myrrh were the gifts given to the Christ child by the Three Kings, along with gold.

rise to the power of Venice, established vast empires, and even shifted the balance of world power. As ambitious European monarchs sought to seize new territory, their brave envoys and explorers set out to discover fresh routes to the spice islands and gold sources of the East, but some found, instead, unknown lands and even entirely new continents. Today's globalization was launched by this hunger for greater power and wealth but the roots of that lay partly in our desire to add flavour and fun to our tables, to ease digestion, to lend our daily lives zest and relish.

In this little volume, we are unable to explore all the myriad spices that beg our attention. The plethora of enticing information has proved a challenge to sift, sort (in alphabetical order of Latin names within each group) and tease into the available pages. But it is a 'taster' – and I hope a tantalizing introduction – to the exotic world of spices in all their appetizing glory. It discovers a feast of remedies, anecdotes, traditional lore, historical adventures and a long-lost era of superstition and magic … Do enjoy the journey!

DISCOVERING THE SPICES

SEEDS

GRAINS OF PARADISE *Aframom melegueta*

Originating in African coastal swamps and once called alligator or Guinea or melegueta pepper, these seeds were transported long ago across the Sahara desert by trade caravans. During the days of the medieval spice trade they were then given their new Paradise name in an attempt to inflate the price by suggesting that these seeds came from the Garden of Eden and floated downriver from Paradise. With handsome, purple, lily-like flowers whose trumpets attract bees and butterflies, their long seedpods are crammed with hundreds of small, red-gold seeds. A ginger relative, the spice was cheaper than true pepper in the Middle Ages, but is much more costly today when it is mainly West Africans and Scandinavians who continue to appreciate this spice.

SOURCES AND USES			
ORIGINS	SPREAD	TASTE TYPE	CULINARY USES
West Africa, including Cameroon and Ghana	Throughout Africa In Europe since at least the 800s A vital cash crop in Ethiopia	Aromatic, spicy and fairly hot More complex than black pepper Citrus hints Hints of jasmine, hazelnut, coriander, ginger and cardamom	Meat, sauces and soups Tunisian stew On potato and green salads, fish, sausages, lemon vinaigrettes On fruit desserts like apple pie and pineapple In beer, wine, gin, rum, brandy

 ### MORE FOOD FACTS

It used to be added to the Roman Hippocras wine.
Its extract can be mixed with butter, honey, peanuts and almonds, and served with after-dinner coffee.
It serves as a dry rub for grilled steaks, chicken thighs and kebabs.
Grains were much appreciated by England's England's Queen Elizabeth I (1533–1603) but King George (1738–1820), banned them, fearing they were being misused in liquor.
A medieval French book said the grains improved stale-smelling wine.

 ### TRADITIONALLY USED FOR

A stimulant, warming agent, digestive aid and diuretic
An aromatic breath freshener
To treat rheumatism (especially in Ghana)

 ### DID YOU KNOW?

West Africa's Pepper (or Grain) Coast is named after this plant.
It is a part of voodoo rites in the Caribbean and Latin America.
It may account for wild lowland gorillas' cardiovascular health – much better in the wild than in captivity.

DILL SEED *Anethum graveolens*

One of the celery family, delicate, feathery dill was used to soothe crying babies; its name derives from Old English *dilla*, meaning 'to lull'. Dill also served as an aphrodisiac and to help resist witchcraft and spells – as recorded in 1627: "Therewith her Vervain and her Dill, that hindereth Witches of their Will." Mentioned in the Bible, dill was a favourite of ancient Egyptians, Greeks and Romans (soldiers would apply burnt dill seeds to their wounds to promote healing). Used in Anglo-Saxon and medieval times for countless ills, it was recorded in the 900s in England by Alfric, Archbishop of Canterbury.

SOURCES AND USES			
ORIGINS	SPREAD	TASTE TYPE	CULINARY USES
South-west Asia and Southern Russia.	Ukraine, Poland, Scandinavia, Germany, Romania, Mediterranean regions and Western Africa	A distinctive pungent, warm taste The seeds provide the strongest flavour Like caraway, but lighter Hints of anise or lemon	With cucumbers, pickles, tomatoes, salmon, trout, soups like borscht, veal, chicken and turkey breast, hard boiled eggs, omelettes, potatoes, rice, peas and beans, mushrooms, cabbage, carrots, seafood, vinegar

 MORE FOOD FACTS

Sprinkle on butter, salads, tomatoes and apple desserts.
Use with sour cream to make cucumber dressing.
It can be added to wine and dips.
Try blending it into tuna salad.
In antiquity dill was added to wine.

 DID YOU KNOW?

Its oil is used in soap-making.
Evil spells (and cramp) can be deterred by drinking dill juice.
Holy Roman Emperor Charlemagne (c.742–814) placed dill
    on banquet tables to control his guests' flatulence
Dill seed is called 'grasshopper's eye' in Arab countries.
It was once kept under lock and key because of its great value.

 TRADITIONALLY USED FOR

Calming and improving sleep
Curing hiccups by boiling dill in wine and inhaling fumes
Soothing babies – and their digestion
Indigestion, colic and hiccups
Stimulating intestine and regulating insulin levels
Gas, bloating, stomach pain
Jaundice, bile and liver problems
Headache, arthritis, inflammation
Boils, ulcers, bad breath
Lack of appetite, nausea
Stimulating milk production
Strengthening nails, bones and brain
It may also prevent certain cancers

CELERY SEED *Apium graveolens*

Celery was first munched by humans some 3,000 years ago. Used by ancient Chinese, Greeks and Romans as a medicine, it was considered both holy and unlucky. In classical Greece the leaves served as garlands for the dead and wreaths for games winners, while its wine was a prize for athletes. In *The Odyssey*, Greek poet Homer describes meadows of violet and wild celery near the cave of the enchantress Calypso. Wild celery is rather bitter so was not valued as a food crop until the 1600s when it was 'tamed' in Italy. Eventually the now-sweeter plant was also persuaded to produce solid rather than hollow stems. Now the stalks and seed – a strong spice – are grown commercially. The seeds are tiny: it takes only one ounce to produce an acre of crop.

SOURCES AND USES			
ORIGINS	**SPREAD**	**TASTE TYPE**	**CULINARY USES**
Mediterranean basin and Middle East	Grown in Northern and Eastern Europe, Egypt, Algeria, India, China, New Zealand, California, Florida, Texas, Michigan, Ohio and southernmost South America Most cultivated seed is from France and India	Aromatic, warm and slightly pungent Salty, a little bitter Aroma like parsley	In bread As a soup base (especially chicken noodle) In casseroles, stews, curries and salad With eggs, fish dishes, cabbage, cilantro, cucumber, fish, capsicum, potatoes, poultry, rice, tomatoes, In appetizers and stuffing, and as a garnish

 TRADITIONALLY USED FOR

Colds, flu and headaches
Toothache and insomnia
Water retention and intestinal gas
Poor digestion and loss of appetite
Arthritis, rheumatism, and gout
Liver and spleen diseases
Reducing muscle spasms, inflammation and menstrual discomfort
Calming nerves, anxiety and hysteria
To increase sexual desire
As a diuretic
The seeds were used in ancient Indian Ayurvedic medicine
    Seed extracts may help lower blood pressure and cholesterol
Roman Aulus Cornelius Celsus described using celery seed in pills to relieve pain in AD 30
Dieters claim that chewing and digesting celery burns ups more calories than in the meal itself

WARNING
Like peanuts, celery can cause severe allergic reactions

 MORE FOOD FACTS

The seeds are ground with salt to make celery salt for
    cooking, cocktails and hot dogs.
To keep celery crisp, soak it in ice-cold water.
A Chelsea Cocktail is a pint of Guinness garnished
    with a celery stick.

 DID YOU KNOW?

In the 1960s, a celebrity at Ambassador East Hotel in
    Chicago was served a Bloody Mary but no swizzle
    stick. He grabbed a stalk of celery from the relish
    tray to stir his cocktail and thus was born the
    celery garnish tradition.
One *Doctor Who* incarnation wore a celery stalk on
    his lapel, claiming it to be an excellent restorative.
Woven garlands of celery leaves were found in
    Tutankhamun's tomb (died 1323 BCE).

MUSTARD *Brassica juncea, B. hirta, B. nigra or Sinapis alba*

The name comes from *must* (young wine) and *ardens* (flaming hot). These tiny, yellowish-white to black seeds provide one of the most widely used spices but do not become pungent until cracked and mixed with liquid. Relished since the Stone Age and cultivated in India from about 3,000 BCE, mustard was the primary spice in Europe long before the spice trade introduced pepper. The Roman writer Pliny the Elder (23–79) advised crushing the seeds in vinegar but Roman diners often simply pounded the seed on their plates and mixed it with wine or water on the spot. Monks planted mustard in vineyards and Pope John XXII (1249–1334) made his useless nephew, who lived near Dijon, his Grand Mustard-Maker: this city soon became the world's mustard centre. The English miller, Jeremiah Colman (made mustard-maker to Queen Victoria in 1866), launched Colman's Mustard in 1814, perfecting the technique of grinding seeds into a fine powder without losing either oil or flavour.

SOURCES AND USES			
ORIGINS	SPREAD	TASTE TYPE	CULINARY USES
Himalayan foothills; first cultivated in India about 3,000 BCE	Via trade routes to Palestine, Egypt, Greece and the Roman world Now mainly produced in Finland, France, Germany, Switzerland, UK, USA	All: hot and spicy Brown: Pungent and bright White (or yellow): More mellow Black: Very strong and distinctive – used in Asian cooking Irish: Whole-grain blended with honey, whiskey and Guinness Prepared mustards include stone-ground, gourmet, Dijon, and wine varieties	In mayonnaise, salad dressings, marinades, vinaigrette, sauces In soups, chillies and sauerkraut With cress, salads, sandwiches, burgers, hot dogs, pretzels, steaks, roast beef, fowl, game, cured meats, sausages, cabbage, root vegetables. Used in pickling, vinegar wine and yeast breads Good with capers and cheese

MORE FOOD FACTS

In Northern India and Nepal the seeds are usually roasted until they pop.

Bruised mustard seeds, mixed with wine, vinegar or lemon juice, create a sweet or spicy paste.

The ancient Sumerians ground mustard to a paste and mixed it with grape juice.

Mustard (mixed with honey or vinegar and cinnamon) used to be stored as balls until the late 1700s when Mrs Clements of Durham invented mustard flour – Durham Mustard.

 ## DID YOU KNOW?

Egypt's King Tutankhamun had supplies in his tomb to take into the afterlife.

Mustardseed is a fairy in William Shakespeare's *A Midsummer Night's Dream*.

Abraham is said to have served cow tongue with mustard.

Jesus's parable of the mustard seed shows how the vast kingdom of God grew from a tiny seed.

An oil made with mustard (plus turpentine, rosemary and camphor) resists frost and damp – so is prized by makers of clocks and precision instruments.

Mustard in hot dogs was launched in 1904 at the St Louis World's Fair, USA.

Mustard flour sprinkled in your socks may prevent frostbite.

Americans use more mustard than any other nationality.

National Mustard Day is celebrated each August in Wisconsin, USA.

The saying, 'Can't cut the mustard' means being unable to face a challenge.

White mustard is used as a green manure.

There are some forty mustard plant species.

Mustard gas is a form of the chemical sulphur; it is not from the plant but is yellow and smells like mustard.

 ## TRADITIONALLY USED FOR

Asthma, sinuses, bronchitis, pneumonia and respiratory disorders, hiccoughs

High blood pressure and circulation

Migraines, neuralgia, toothache

Aching muscles

Rheumatoid arthritis, neck cricks

Bruises, hair loss, chilblains, colic

Spasms, epilepsy

Stimulating appetite and digestion

Soothing digestive problems

Warming footbaths and mustard poultices

Sterilizing, deodorizing and as an antiseptic

Scorpion stings and snake bites

Monks mixed it with crayfish powder to spread on wounds

Nutrients in mustard seeds may prevent upset stomach and colon cancer growth

It is good for snake and mushroom poison, if taken promptly

In Maharashtra, India, mustard-oil massages warm the body during extreme winters

CORIANDER or CILANTRO *Coriandrum sativum*

These slightly sweet, citrus-tasting seeds have been enjoyed for some 7,000 years and were placed in the tomb of the Egyptian pharaoh Tutankhamen for his afterlife pleasure. The Vikings sampled the aromatic spice during their raids on Constantinople and took it back to Scandinavia. In the Han Dynasty in China (207 BCE–220 CE) coriander was considered an aid to immortality and an aphrodisiac – which may have led to its inclusion in *The Arabian Nights* tales. It was also grown by Puritans in the British-American colonies but perhaps not for that reason!

SOURCES AND USES			
ORIGINS	**SPREAD**	**TASTE TYPE**	**CULINARY USES**
Mediterranean and Middle East	Southern Europe, North Africa, southern Asia Large-fruited types (used for ground and blended spices) grow in tropical countries like Morocco, India and Australia. Smaller fruit grow in temperate regions and usually have a higher volatile oil content	Slightly sweet, citrus-tasting Grassy, lemony and fresh Roots have a deeper, more intense flavour	The seeds feature in Mediterranean, Scandinavian, Middle Eastern, Caribbean, Brazilian, Mexican, Latin American, African, Chinese, Southeast Asian and Indian (here called dhania) cuisines Complements chicken, lamb, pork, Indian curries, peas, fish, shrimps, fruit, pickled vegetables, rye bread and sausages The seeds are sometimes used in beer brewing Roasted ones are eaten as a snack

 MEDICAL APPLICATIONS

Coriander has antioxidant properties and can delay food spoilage.
Its diuretic properties and insulin-like activity may control mild diabetes.
Its essential oils serve as an aphrodisiac and cure temporary impotency.
Vets used coriander as a drug for cattle and horses.

 TRADITIONALLY USED FOR

Toothache
Urinary tract infections, soothing hemorrhoids
Improving digestion and appetite
Joint and muscle problems
Inhibiting fungal infections
Weight loss
As a laxative

 DID YOU KNOW?

The name of Ariadne, daughter of King Minos of Crete, may have evolved from the plant's Mycenaean Greek name, *koriadnon*.
Greek koris means bed bug: both bugs and coriander contain aldehydes – and smell alike.
Coriander flourished in the Hanging Gardens of Babylon.
It is used in distilling gin.
Sugarplums (the inspiration for Pyotr Ilyich Tchaikovsky's Sugar Plum Fairy in The Nutcracker ballet were sugar-coated coriander.
Ancient Hebrews included it in their Passover meal.
Spanish conquistadors introduced it to Mexico and Peru.
It is one of the oldest essential oils, mentioned in 1574 Berlin price lists.
Mrs Lovett in Stephen Sondheim's Sweeney Todd musical advised ". … being careful with your coriander, that's what makes the gravy grander."

CUMIN *Cuminum cyminum*

This parsley family member has small white or pink flowers in umbels and ridged oblong yellow-brown seeds with oil canals. Cultivated for some 4,000 years, cumin is mentioned in the Bible as both seasoning and the currency for paying priest tithes. Its antifungal qualities helped mummify Egyptian pharaohs. Ancient Greeks kept it handy on the dining table, just as Moroccans do today. By the Middle Ages, cumin had mutated into a love symbol: wedding guests kept it in their pockets and soldiers went to war with a loaf of cumin bread baked by their wives.

SOURCES AND USES			
ORIGINS	**SPREAD**	**TASTE TYPE**	**CULINARY USES**
Egypt, Turkmenistan and east Mediterranean	To India (now the major exporter); also Syria, Turkey, China, Iran, Tajikistan, Turkey, Morocco, Mexico, Chile, Iran, India, Sicily and Malta	Nutty, peppery, slightly bitter. Warm tinge left on tongue. Black cumin is sweeter and milder	Features in South Asian, North African, Persian, Mexican and Latin American cuisines. In curry and chilli powder blends. Kormas, masalas, stews, soups, spiced gravies and sauces. With beef, lamb, poultry, fish, avocados, beans, cabbage, cucumber, roast potatoes, hard cheese, rice, pickles, bread (especially in France) and tomatoes. Dust on chocolate and pastries

 MORE FOOD FACTS

In ancient Greece and Rome, cumin's peppery taste made it a substitute for expensive black pepper.

 DID YOU KNOW?

Cumin was introduced to the Americas by Spanish and Portuguese colonists.

India produces 70 per cent of the world's cumin, eating 90 per cent of its own output (63 per cent of the world's cumin).

Cumin is often in birdseed mixes.

It was a symbol of avarice in ancient Rome; greedy emperors Marcus Aurelius and Antoninus Pius were nicknamed after it.

In the Middle Ages it was thought that cumin kept chickens (and lovers) from wandering.

 TRADITIONALLY USED FOR

Improving digestion and nutrient assimilation

Anaemia, the common cold

Enhancing appetite and taste

Vision, strength, lactation

Fever, diarrhoea, vomiting

Edema, puerperal disorders

Heart disease, flatulence

It boosts cancer prevention, especially stomach or liver tumours

Antidiabetic, immunologic, anti-epileptic, antitumour and antimicrobial

A paste of ground cumin, pepper and honey is said to be an aphrodisiac

Excellent source of iron, calcium, copper, potassium, manganese, selenium, zinc and magnesium

CARDAMOM *Elettaria cardamomum* and *Amonum subulatum*

With its intense floral fragrance, this is the third most expensive spice in the world, after saffron and vanilla. In the fourth century BCE, Greek's father of botany, Theophratus, identified *Elettaria* with light green pods (white if bleached) and *Amomum*, hotter and best with savoury dishes. Their papery outer shells enclose small black seeds. Ancient Egyptians used cardomom for medicines, rituals, embalming and cleaning their teeth. Assyrians, Babylonians, Greeks and Romans recognized its virtues in perfumes, ointments and aromatic oils. The Vikings discovered it in Constantinople and took it back to Scandinavia – where it remains popular.

SOURCES AND USES			
ORIGINS	SPREAD	TASTE TYPE	CULINARY USES
Southern India and Pakistan	Northern Persia and Greece Then India, Bhutan, Nepal, Pakistan and Sri Lanka Guatemala now main producer and exporter	Strong, citrusy, aromatic and resinous Elettaria: cool minty tang Amomum: hotter, camphor-like, smoky	Soup, rice, curry, meats and meatballs, beans, pastries, desserts, fruits, sweet breads, cakes, chocolate, porridge, spiced and herbal teas, liqueurs and ice cream Blends with ginger and turmeric, allspice, pepper, cinnamon, cloves, fennel, paprika and saffron

 ## MORE FOOD FACTS

Scandinavians use it in Christmas 'glogg' mulled wine.
Seeds should be powdered only when ready to use, or the aroma vanishes.
In Egypt they are ground and put in coffee.
In the East Indies they serve as a condiment and for chewing with betel.

 ## DID YOU KNOW?

Ancient Egyptians chewed the pods to clean teeth and freshen breath.
The seeds can be chewed too; the Wrigley company incorporated cardamom into its chewing gum to neutralize breath odours.
The Cardamom Hills in India drew their name from the spice prolifically growing wild there.

 ## TRADITIONALLY USED FOR

Throat, teeth and gum infections
Congestion of the lungs and TB
Eyelid inflammation
Asthma and heat stroke
Snake and scorpion bites
Constipation, dysentery
Breaking up kidney and gall stones
It is an ingredient in the traditional medicine of China, India (Ayurveda), Pakistan, Japan, Korea, Nepal, and Vietnam
This is a cure for overindulgence and other digestion problems

FENNEL SEED *Foeniculum vulgare*

With its feathery leaves and golden flowers, fennel is both herb and spice as all parts are edible. It was used by the ancient Greeks and spread throughout Europe by Imperial Rome. Pliny observed that serpents ate fennel when casting their old skins and sharpened their sight by rubbing against it. One of the nine plants in the Anglo Saxon's *Nine Herbs Charm*, it was an essential in medieval monks' medicinal gardens. Somewhat later, American Puritans chewed it during long church services to stop hunger pangs and tummy rumbles.

SOURCES AND USES			
ORIGINS	SPREAD	TASTE TYPE	CULINARY USES
Mediterranean	India and Persia Now from Norway to Asia, Australia, South America and USA	Like anise or liquorice	Fennel looks like celery but tastes like anise or liquorice Enriches soups, stews, sauces, bread, pickles, liqueurs, absinthe Good with fish (especially salmon and mackerel) Gives Italian sausages their special flavour It complements fish (especially salmon and mackerel)

MORE FOOD FACTS

The seeds feature in Indian, Asian and Middle Eastern cooking.
They are an ingredient in Chinese five spice.
It was added to salted fish during Lent.

DID YOU KNOW?

In ancient times fennel was said to make you strong and improve your eyesight.
It was gown on Holy Roman Emperor Charlemagne's imperial farms.
Later it flavoured sack, a popular mead drink.
On Midsummer's Eve fennel was draped over doors to ward off evil.
Fennel eases dog flatulence and deters fleas in kennels.

TRADITIONALLY USED FOR

Yellow jaundice, gout and cramp
Wheezing and bronchial spasms
Hiccups, wind, nausea
Stomach muscles, intestines
Improving longevity and urine output
Serpent bites, mushroom poisoning
Eyewashes and eye cataracts.
Gripe water for colicky babies
Increasing a mother's milk
Aromatic fennel oil sweetens candies, cordials, liqueur, soap and perfume
Nibbling the seeds refreshes the breath and improves digestion
Nicholas Culpeper (1616-54) said that fennel in broth makes '…people more lean that are too fat'

SUNFLOWER SEEDS *Helianthus annuus*

Possibly domesticated even earlier than corn, these tall stately plants, beloved by honey bees, can shoot 3.7 metres (12 feet) tall in one summer, producing up to 2,000 seeds. The Aztecs revered them; they depicted their glories in their temples of the Sun where priestesses carried and were crowned with the flowers. Early European explorers in the Americas duly despatched the flowers they so admired back to Europe, from where they spread to other continents, too. Visiting Holland, Tzar Peter the Great of Russia became enamoured with them and took seeds back to Russia … in due course over two million Russian acres a year would be dedicated to sunflower oil production.

SOURCES AND USES			
ORIGINS	SPREAD	TASTE TYPE	CULINARY USES
Mexico and Peru	Around the world Thrive from the Rocky Mountains to tropical parts of the Americas Commercial crops: Ukraine, Russia, Argentina, China, France, Romania, Bulgaria, Turkey, Hungary and USA Oil: produced in Russia – plus Rumania, Hungary, Bulgaria and Poland	Sweet and crunchy Black ones are pressed for oil Striped seeds are eaten	Healthy snacks and garnishes To make spreads or flour Add to breads Sprouted seeds are added to salads Boil young buds and serve like artichokes

MORE FOOD FACTS

In Turkey, Syria and Israel freshly roasted seeds are popular.
Native Americans ground them into flour for cakes, bread or
    a mash with beans, squash and corn.
They are often sold as feed for both wild and pet birds.

TRADITIONALLY USED FOR

Bronchial or pulmonary problems
Colds, whooping cough, fevers, ague
Snakebites, soothing ointments
Malaria sufferers in the Caucasus are wrapped in sunflower
    leaves and damp cloth

DID YOU KNOW?

Its purple dye is used for body painting and textiles.
Hard dried stalks serve as a building material or fuel.
Dutch artist Vincent van Gogh did a series of paintings
    featuring sunflowers.
The tallest sunflower, in the Netherlands in 1986, reached
    7.75 metres (25 feet).
The stems contain a fibre used in making paper.
The seeds are often munched by US baseball players.

FLAX SEED or LINSEED *Linum usitatissimum*

Flax has delicate, pale-blue or turquoise flowers. It is the source of one of the first commercial oils and linen cloth. Both seeds and the woven cloth have been found in Egyptian tombs (mummies were wrapped in linen – as was Christ's body in the tomb). Flanders became the major centre for flax in the Middle Ages. In time, flax fibres – twice as strong as cotton – were used for lamp-wicks, ropes, cord, sailcloth, canvas, sheets, fish-nets, thread, bowstrings, bandages, webbing, paints, varnish, bank note and cigarette paper, teabags, printing inks, linoleum, cattle feed, candlewicks, sacks, bags and purses.

SOURCES AND USES			
ORIGINS	**SPREAD**	**TASTE TYPE**	**CULINARY USES**
Switzerland, Germany, China and India	Temperate and tropical regions	Nutty, slightly spicy	Flax seed sprouts are edible In India, flaxseed is roasted, powdered, and eaten with boiled rice A little of the oil will enhance potatoes and some cheeses

 DID YOU KNOW?

Bundles of flax fibre look like blonde hair, hence the saying 'flaxen locks'.
The girl with the flaxen hair is one of French composer Claude Debussy's most recorded pieces.
Spun and dyed flax fibres have been found from 30,000 years ago.
Linseed and corn bread was made by Ancient Greeks and Romans but caused flatulence.
In early versions of Sleeping Beauty, the princess pricks her finger on a sliver of flax.
The flowers offer protection against sorcery.
Oil from the ripened dried seed helps create wood finishes, oil paint binder, glazing putty hardener and gun-stock (or cricket-bat) coating.
It is used in gold-leaf gilding and to protect billiards and wooden musical instruments.
It helps bind together particles that create linoleum.
It makes linocuts for printmaking.

 TRADITIONALLY USED FOR

Lowering blood pressure
Respiratory issues, pleurisy
Burns, scalds, eye problems
Cold, flu, fever, coughs
Rheumatism or gout
Breast and prostrate cancers
Abscesses and boils
Constipation, gravel, stone
A crushed seed poultice (plus lobelia seed) allays irritation and pain
Flax seeds may lower cholesterol levels
Linseed tea (with honey and lemon) soothes colds, coughs and urinary irritation

 WARNING Eating the plant or oil in large quantities can lead to bowel obstruction, breathing problems, convulsions and even paralysis. Skin contact with linseed oil may cause irritation.

NUTMEG AND **MACE** *Myristica fragrans*

Yellow, pear-like fruits contain a single, wrinkled, egg-shaped nutmeg; mace is this seed's bright scarlet, lacy covering that can be ground into coarse powder. Until the 1700s, the only source of these 'twin' spices was Indonesia but exactly where nutmegs grew was kept secret from Europeans until 1621 when the Dutch massacred and enslaved Banda islanders and so were able to control nutmeg production – a rich prize. The invaders established a fiercely protected monopoly, sending out war-vessels to destroy trees planted elsewhere. They even coated nutmegs in caustic lime to prevent sprouting so no client could cultivate their own – a policy undermined by local pigeons who deposited the seeds in their droppings as they flew from one island to another!

SOURCES AND USES			
ORIGINS	**SPREAD**	**TASTE TYPE**	**CULINARY USES**
The Moluccas (Indonesian Spice Islands)	Caribbean Grenada, Sumatra, French Guiana, India (including Kerala) and Malaysia When the British controlled the Banda Islands, they transplanted nutmegs to Sri Lanka, Penang, Sumatra and Singapore Main producers now: Indonesia and Grenada	Nutmeg is slightly sweeter Mace is more delicate – ideal in light dishes	Grate nutmeg into soups and stews Mace and nutmeg improve potato dishes, dumplings, meatloaf, Scottish haggis, soups, sauces, Brussels sprouts, cauliflower, string beans, rice, jam, nutmeg butter, mulled cider, wine, eggnog and rum punch

MORE FOOD FACTS

Shred, blend – or boil rind (to make nutmeg juice).
Add nutmeg to sweet and savoury Indian dishes.
Nutmeg is the main pumpkin pie spice.
Nutmeg features in squash recipes.

WARNING Myristicin poisoning can cause convulsions, palpitations, nausea and delirium – and poison your dog; nutmeg is banned in Saudi Arabia.

 TRADITIONALLY USED FOR

Reducing scars and acne
Digestive problems and flatulence
Pestilence and putrid fevers
Improving blood circulation and warmth
Kidney infections, nausea, vomiting
Pain relief, coughs
Strengthening liver, as a sleep aid
Antibacterial properties protect teeth and gums
It may shield the brain against Alzheimer's
Its essential oil relieves muscular and joint pain
In the 1800s, it was used to cause abortions, overdoses
    sometimes leading to nutmeg poisoning
Nutmeg is a stimulant and tonic – good for
    convalescents
Grated nutmeg mixed with lard makes a fine ointment
    for piles

 DID YOU KNOW?

Muslim sailors, including fictional Sinbad the Sailor, knew
    nutmeg as a valuable commodity.
In the 1500s, nutmeg was said to ward off the plague;
    demand increased and its price rocketed.
The spice is used as snuff in Indonesia and India.
Nutmeg can be intoxicating, producing euphoria, and in the
    1960s was named as an 'alternative high' on US college
    campuses.
Nutmeg trees cannot be harvested for seven years or so – and
    do not reach full production until twenty years old.
Ground nutmeg is smoked in India.
Its essential oils are in cosmetic and pharmaceutical products
    such as toothpaste.

POPPY SEEDS *Papaver somniferum*

Since antiquity, poppies have symbolized honour and fertility. Many civilizations believed bountiful crops thrived in poppy-dotted fields and the scarlet blooms with tiny, nutritious, kidney-shaped seeds have been harvested since 5000 BCE. They flourished in Mesopotamia, were found in the tombs of ancient Egyptians, were used by the Greeks as a bread flavouring and for medicine, while in Crete, the Minoans cultivated them for opium. Medieval Europeans used the seeds on bread, to improve fertility, wealth and sleep and for magical invisibility. Poppy's roaring trade culminated in the Opium Wars in China. The seed can lie dormant for over eighty years; an estimated 2,500 poppy seeds per square foot were brought to the surface in World War One battlefields; soon sheets of scarlet spread across no man's land and on graves – to become a symbol of war sorrow.

SOURCES AND USES			
ORIGINS	**SPREAD**	**TASTE TYPE**	**CULINARY USES**
Ancient Egypt	Arab traders took poppies across Greece and the Orient, Persia, Khorasan and India Now a commercial crop in Pakistan, Spain, France, Turkey, Israel, East Europe, Holland, the Czech Republic, India and Australia	Nutty	Sprinkle on breads, cakes, muffins, strudels, pastry, crackers, pasta, pancakes and waffles Popular in Indian, Jewish, German and Slavic cooking Use ground on egg noodles, fish, vegetable dishes, fruit salad dressings, and to thicken sauces

 TRADITIONALLY USED FOR

Insomnia, offering rest and sleep to the sick and weak
Soothing nervous irritability
Cough mixtures, expectorants, catarrh, sore throats, voice loss
Head pains, toothache, general pain relief
Inflammation, consumption, gout
St Anthony's fire, falling-sickness, pleurisy, ague
Easing belly flux and women's courses

DID YOU KNOW?

A single bagel covered with poppy seeds can produce a false positive test for morphine and codeine.

Common names include Flanders poppy, corn rose, redweed and Shirley poppies.

A poppy goddess was worshipped in Minoan Crete.

Early Greeks may have used poppy extracts as a form of euthanasia.

Red corn poppy flowers symbolize love in Persian literature.

Papaver somniferum seeds are banned in Singapore and Saudi Arabia because of their morphine content.

 ### OTHER USES

Rich in *oleic* and *linoleic* acids, poppy seeds help lower 'bad' and increase 'good' cholesterol levels, preventing coronary artery disease and strokes

They are a potential source of anti-cancer drugs

The ancient Greek physician Hippocrates (460–377 BCE) described the juice as narcotic, hypnotic and cathartic

Today, poppy morphine and codeine are vital medical drugs

 ### MORE FOOD FACTS

The seeds can be ground into a paste for cooking or to be used as a skin moisturiser.

Poppy-seed oil is an olive oil substitute and has multiple culinary, industrial and medicinal uses.

Traditional Slovakian and Lithuanian Christmas Eve meals include yeast biscuits soaked in poppy seed 'milk'.

Birds enjoy poppy seeds.

PARSLEY SEED *Petroselinum crispum*

Tiny, oval-shaped parsley seeds, all furrowed and ribbed, are often slow to germinate and one seventeenth-century superstition claimed that 'Parsley seed goes nine times to the Devil' before springing to life. The ancient Greeks used it for ceremonial purposes, believing it arose from the blood of hero Archemorus after he was slain by a dragon, and the Romans introduced it into every nation they ruled. Anglo-Saxons employed parsley to repair battle-fractured skulls but parsley is toxic to many birds and animals and its oil should never be given to pregnant women … goldfinches, however, love the seeds.

SOURCES AND USES			
ORIGINS	**SPREAD**	**TASTE TYPE**	**CULINARY USES**
Sardinia	Italy, Algeria, Tunisia, then across Europe	Sweet, aromatic, anise-like Spikes taste and adds zest	Very sparingly with cheese

 DID YOU KNOW?

Holy Roman Emperor Charlemagne adored cheese flavored with parsley seeds.
A French remedy for scrofulous swellings is green parsley and snails.
Whoever can grow parsley is said to be head of the household – or a witch.
Parsley represses odours; corpses were sprinkled with it to reduce the stench.

 TRADITIONALLY USED FOR

Diarrhoea, flatulence, indigestion, constipation, stomach pain, gall stones
Rheumatism, sciatica
Menstrual pain, flow, regularity; nurtures female reproductive organs
Inducing abortions
Promotes estrogen secretion
Libido loss, prostate issues
High blood pressure
Uurinary or kidney disorders, fluid retention, cystitis
Coughs, haemorrhoids
Wounds, gum problems, ulcers
Jaundice, colic
Heals foot-rot in goats and sheep

 OTHER USES

Parsley seeds contain more volatile oil than the root, and are an excellent remedy for ague and malarial disorders
It is antiseptic and a gentle diuretic
It may help resist cancer, asthma and diabetes
In the trenches of the First World War, parsley tea relieved dysentery's kidney complications
It is in many face cleansing oils, toners and eye creams

 WARNING

Parsley contains myristicin; in *large* amounts, this may cause hallucinations, nausea, and vomiting. Pregnant women should avoid the seeds.

ANISE (ANISEED) *Pimpinella anisum*

Cultivated for at least 2,000 years and mentioned in the Bible, this member of the carrot family has delicate, yellow or white flowers, small, brown, hairy seeds and a gentle, sweet aroma. Highly prized anise was used for offerings, tithes, and payment of taxes in Palestine, and enjoyed by ancient Egyptians as early as 1500 BCE. In the ninth century the Holy Roman Emperor Charlemagne commanded that anise be grown on the imperial farms. The seeds are said to avert evil and to entice spirits to help with spells.

SOURCES AND USES			
ORIGINS	SPREAD	TASTE TYPE	CULINARY USES
Eastern Mediterranean region (Crete, Middle East and Southwest Asia)	Central Europe and many warmer regions Now grown commercially in Russia, Bulgaria, Germany, Malta, Spain, Italy, North Africa and Greece	Sweet and spicy	Anise flavours cakes, biscuits and rye bread Use with fish, poultry, root vegetables and in soups Also in black jelly beans, liquorice, aniseed balls and humbugs DRINKS It is in Greek ouzo, French absinthe, ainisette and pastis, German Jägermeister and Italian Sambuca It is added to some root beers Anise may be one of the secret ingredients in French Chartreuse

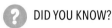 **DID YOU KNOW?**

To avoid flatulence, the Romans served anise-spiced cakes after a rich meal or wedding feast – thus giving rise to the wedding cake tradition.

Anise oil is an effective bait in rat or mouse traps.

Beekeepers use anise to encourage bees to return to their hives.

An aniseed pillow may prevent nightmares.

The seeds attract dogs and are used to lay drag hunt trails (or to disrupt hounds in anti-blood sport demonstrations).

Aniseed oil capsules were set in steam locomotive bearings; their distinctive smell warned of overheating.

 TRADITIONALLY USED FOR

Snake bites, head lice, mites and biting insects

Low libido, erectile problems

Digestive issues, flatulence, colic, dropsy, bowel problems

Bad breath, hiccups, hard, dry coughs

Falling sickness, convulsions

Insomnia

Intestinal problems in horses or dogs

Menstrual cramps

Stimulates milk production

Gently provoking urine

Mixed with lard or whale oil to soothe skin irritations

SESAME SEED *Sesamum indicum*

Although it was known in Africa and the Middle East from very early on, the word *indicum* in sesame's Latin name means 'coming from India', and it was certainly mentioned in very early Hindu legends. This oldest known oilseed crop (it was included in the spice list of the Egyptian Ebers Papyrus that dates back about three and a half thousand years), an Assyrian myth of about 3000 BCE claimed that the gods drank sesame wine just before creating the Earth. Ancient Chinese burned its oil as a light source and used its soot for ink-blocks and calligraphy. Sesame oil lamps were lit in Babylon from 2100 to 1750 BCE when women also used sesame as a perfume base and ate the seeds mixed with honey to prolong beauty and youth; Roman soldiers ate the same confection to attain strength and energy! Sesame was worth its weight in gold during the Middle Ages and many ancient presses for its oil survived in the Middle East. *'Open sesame'* (Ali Baba's password which revealed the robber's treasure) was inspired by how ripe sesame pods explode open at the lightest touch, shooting out their buff, gold, tan or black seeds.

SOURCES AND USES			
ORIGINS	**SPREAD**	**TASTE TYPE**	**CULINARY USES**
India or East Africa	Turkey, Middle East, East Indies, then Asia, especially Myanmar and Japan	Nutty and aromatic	Ground into flour or added whole to bread, rolls, bagels, crackers, savoury sticks
	African slaves called them *benné seeds* and took them to America		Used in salads, soups, noodle dishes
	Now grows in most tropical, subtropical, and southern temperate regions		With smoked fish, lobster, chicken, pork, vegetables
	Some 3.84 million metric tonnes are harvested a year; the main exporter Myanmar produces over 722,900 metric tonnes of seeds (18.84 per cent of world production), followed by India and Mexico.		In butter, shortening, margarine
			Cakes, muffins, confectionary bars and balls, cookies, wafers, desserts, ice cream and chocolate
	Largest importer is Japan; then China, USA, Canada, Netherlands, Turkey and France. 75 per cent of Mexican sesame production is bought by the McDonald's hamburger chain		The paste is added to sauces

 MORE FOOD FACTS

Both seeds and oil are vital in Chinese cuisine.
Sesame oil is the main cooking fat in Korea and China –
   equivalent to olive oil in Mediterranean cuisine.
The oil flavours dips and marinades.
Sweet nougat is a Sicilian (albeit originally Arabian)
   Christmas dessert; sesame seeds are fused with honey
   and served on orange leaves.

 TRADITIONALLY USED FOR

Diabetes
Cancer
Multiple sclerosis
Huntington's disease
Stress, headaches, migraines
Iron deficiency anaemia, high cholesterol, blood pressure
Constipation
PMS symptoms
Intestinal parasites
Sexual prowess
Promoting heart, bone, teeth and skin health
Detoxifying the body

 OTHER USES

The Chinese use black sesame seed to retain youthful health.
Massaging with the oil helps circulation, soothes the nervous
   system and relieves stress.

 DID YOU KNOW?

The Guinness Book of Records lists the world's longest
   poem ever written on a sesame seed (28 Chinese
   characters), executed by miniature artist Chen Forng-
   shean (born in 1956).
Cantonese black sesame sweet soup *(tong sui)* may stop
   hair going grey.
Sesame crops cope with deserts, drought, high heat and
   monsoon rains.
In India, the seeds are sacred, a symbol of immortality
   placed in funeral vases.
Egyptian images show sesame being sprinkled on dough
   by bakers; seeds were found in Tutankhamun's tomb.
A Korean dish, *sannakji*, comprises live octopuses cut and
   served with sesame seed oil; sometimes still-moving
   tentacles dangerously stick to diners' throats!
Massaging a baby with sesame oil helps it sleep.
It is an ingredient in soaps, lubricants and cosmetics.

FENUGREEK *Trigonella foenum-graecum*

Fenugreek grows in sandy, seaside tracts or dry riverbeds. Also known as wild clover and, indeed, smelling like clover, brownish-gold seeds in long, narrow pods follow dainty, yellow-white flowers. The Greeks added fenugreek (meaning 'Greek hay') to improve their livestock's hay but carbon dating on charred seeds indicate that it was being used long before, about 4000 BCE in Iraq. Ancient Egyptians certainly ate it as well as adding it to their holy incense when embalming the dead; desiccated seeds were found in Tutankhamen's tomb. Jews defending Jerusalem mixed fenugreek with boiling oil to ward off Roman invaders.

SOURCES AND USES			
ORIGINS	**SPREAD**	**TASTE TYPE**	**CULINARY USES**
The Middle East (especially Iraq and Egypt)	France, Spain, Turkey, Morocco, Iran, Afghanistan, Bangladesh, Nepal, Pakistan, India, China and Argentina Main producer is now India (Rajasthan supplies over 80 per cent of the country's output)	Strongly-scented; semi-bitter Like lovage or celery with burnt sugar	Indian curries, dal Pickles, mango chutney and marinades Turkish, Egyptian, Iranian and Ethiopian dishes Baked goods, bread, pitta bread Candy, ice cream, chewing gum, soft drinks Butterscotch and rum flavourings Imitation vanilla or maple syrup

 ## MORE FOOD FACTS

Herbal tea can be made from the seeds, and roasted seeds make a coffee substitute.

They can be sprouted for salads and vegetable dishes.

Fenugreek is in the Jewish version of *halva* confectionary and is in *hilbeh* sauce at Jewish New Year celebrations.

 ## DID YOU KNOW?

Women (especially in harems) ate fenugreek to gain weight and enlarge their breasts.

The Roman historian Cato the Elder (234–149 BCE) listed it as a cattle-feed crop.

'May you tread in peace the soil where fenugreek grows' is an Arabic greeting.

It is a yellow dye and is used as an insect repellent in grain storage.

 ## TRADITIONALLY USED FOR

Common cold, sore throats
Stomach, intestine and kidney problems
Abscesses, boils, carbuncles
Scrofula, rickets, malaria, anaemia
Diabetes, gout
Senility
PMS and menopause symptoms
An aphrodisiac, increasing male libido
Condition powders for horses and cattle
Flavouring cattle foods and hay
Improving muscle strength for weight-lifting
Steroids, oral contraceptives
Stimulating breast milk production

FRUITS AND BERRIES

CHILLI AND CAYENNE *Capsicum annuum*

The many varieties of chilli peppers of the *Capsicum annuum* family have been enjoyed in the Americas since at least 7500 BCE and were certainly being cultivated over 6,000 years ago in Mexico. The Spanish and Portuguese discovered red chilli peppers in the Americas in the sixteenth century and brought them back home to Europe, where they were first cultivated by monks. Cayenne chilli fruits are long pods that change colour – green and yellow when unripe but bright red once fully mature with small flat seeds inside. Cayenne pepper, also known as Guinea spice, red hot chilli pepper and bird pepper, is the well-ground, red powder of the dried pods and seeds, and is very hot – it is used to flavour dishes and for medicinal purposes.

SOURCES AND USES			
ORIGINS	SPREAD	TASTE TYPE	CULINARY USES
Central and South America (French Guiana)	Portugal, Spain and Morocco, then India, Central Asia, Korea and Turkey India is the world's largest producer, consumer and exporter of chilli Andhra Pradesh produces 75 per cent of India's chilli exports Chilli was brought to Japan by Portuguese missionaries in 1542	*C. annuum* includes the sweet bell pepper or capsicums, but many chillies can be very hot and piquant	Often combined with vinegar Hot sauces Chilli con carne Indonesian, Korean and Chinese (Sichuan) cooking Spanish chorizo, Indian tandoori chicken Chilli powder mix includes dried ground chilli peppers (often both cayenne and paprika), cumin, garlic, and oregano With beef and beans In stews, soups, sausages, tomato sauces Cayenne is usually found in buffalo wing sauce

 MORE FOOD FACTS

Chillies can be dried or pickled.
Its phosphorus, magnesium, potassium and iron improve heart health.

 DID YOU KNOW?

The irritant capsaicin extracted from chillies is used in pepper sprays.
Chillies make an effective crop defense against elephants.
Birds have a lessened sensitivity to chilli so it can be used to protect birdseed from mammal theft!
US presidents George Washington and Thomas Jefferson are both known to have grown chillies.

 TRADITIONALLY USED FOR

Dilating blood vessels
Improving blood circulation and regulating high blood pressure
Increasing oxygen and energy levels
Regulating digestive system and long-term weight loss
As an aphrodisiac
For pain relief
Promoting healthy liver function and tissue production (with its phosphorus, magnesium, potassium and iron)

PAPRIKA (RED PEPPER) *Capsicum annuum*

Paprika is made from fruits of the red pepper, one of many members of the chilli pepper *Capsicum annuum* family. Native to South and Central America, chillies were brought to Europe in the sixteenth century by the Spanish and Portuguese, and soon Spanish monks were cultivating distinct varieties, including one that they called pimenton. Transported across the continent, it became known as paprika in Hungary. The dried and ground spice, which can be very hot, became a vital element of Hungarian cuisine when in the 1920s a horticulturist there bred a somewhat milder variety. Sweet paprika has more than half of the seeds removed; hot paprika contains more seeds, plus stalks. The sweet, red (tomato) pepper is the main paprika source and Hungarians fiercely guard their 'red gold' plants – giving these twice the acreage of other crops.

SOURCES AND USES			
ORIGINS	**SPREAD**	**TASTE TYPE**	**CULINARY USES**
Central and South America	Portugal, Spain and Morocco Hungary, Serbia, the Netherlands, South America and California	Ripe and sweet if grown in sun Flavours vary from one nation to another Spanish paprika can be smoked over oak The bright red Hungarian paprika has a unique, sweeter taste	Hungarian goulash Spanish chorizo With sausages, beef, stews, grilled meats, seafood, meatloaf, beans, eggs, rice, soups, vegetables, stuffing, tomato sauces Seasoning mashed, roast and fried potatoes In Moroccan cuisine, paprika may be blended with little olive oil

 MORE FOOD FACTS

Tables in Hungary are set with salt and hot-paprika shakers (*not* pepper).
The international spice trade is in *whole* spices; *ground* paprika is the exception.
If mixed into flamingo feed in zoos, paprika keeps the birds' feathers pink.
It contains vitamins A, E and K.
Its phosphorus, magnesium, potassium and iron improve heart health.
Hungarian scientist Dr Albert Szent-Györgyi won a Nobel Prize in 1937 for his research on paprika; he found it has a higher content of vitamin C than citrus fruit – seven times more than oranges.
Chillies can be dried or pickled.

 TRADITIONALLY USED FOR

Blood vessels and circulation
Energizing and stimulating
Reducing depression, lethargy, tiredness
Arthritis
Headaches

 DID YOU KNOW?

Kaloscsa in Hungary hosts an annual Paprika Festival and Harvest Ball.
Paprika dyes hair red.
The explorer Christopher Columbus dubbed the plants peppers because of their spicy hot taste – a substitute for the condiment pepper.

CARAWAY SEEDS *Carum carvi*

Caraway has small, feathery leaves and creamy flowers in umbels. Its long, brown, crescent-shaped seeds are actually fruits and have been garnered since prehistoric times – caraway seeds have been found in Stone Age settlements. The harvested plants are usually left in bundles to dry in sunlight. In the Levant it flavours *harissa*, a chilli paste that, among its many uses, is served to mark a new baby's arrival. Caraway was once thought to protect children from witches and to prevent fickle lovers straying, and so became an ingredient of love potions. It was also said to keep fowls from wandering – certainly homing pigeons enjoy the seeds.

SOURCES AND USES			
ORIGINS	**SPREAD**	**TASTE TYPE**	**CULINARY USES**
Southern Europe	Finland and the Netherlands plus east and southeast Europe, North Africa (including Egypt), western Asia, Canada and the USA Finland supplies some 28 per cent of the world's caraway	Aromatic; warm, sweet undertones Bitter, sharp, nutty Pairs well with garlic Root tastes like parsnip Pungent, anise-like flavour	An after-meal delicacy In casseroles, bread (especially rye), desserts German sauerkraut, sausages, dumplings Indian meals Liqueurs, Scandinavian aquavit, cordials, port British seed cake, baked fruit With pork, goose, cabbage, cheese Scattered over cakes or scones Add young shoots to salads Boil roots as a vegetable

MORE FOOD FACTS

Caraway is a rich source of dietary fibre.
It contains iron, copper, calcium, potassium, manganese, selenium, zinc, magnesium, plus
vitamins A, E and C, as well as thiamin, pyridoxine, riboflavin and niacin.
Mixed with milk and made into bread, it was eaten by Roman soldiers.
In the 1500s, caraway was a condiment.
Tender spring leaves can be boiled in soup.

TRADITIONALLY USED FOR

Indigestion, flatulence, colic
Colds, earache, bruises
Constipation, hysteria
Stimulating milk production
Flavouring children's medicines
Improving the memory
Protecting against cancers, infection and ageing
A breath freshener

DID YOU KNOW?

Caraway adds fragrance to perfumes, lotions and soaps.
It prevented theft and kept thieves from escaping (any object containing caraway could not be stolen).
In Germany, a dish of caraway seeds under children's beds protected them from witches.

CITRUS ZEST (usually orange, lime, grapefruit, lemon or citron) *Citrus*

Citrus trees thrive in sunny, frost-free conditions. The strong-flavoured zest is the outer peel (or epicarp) which contains sacs of excellent aromatic oils. This rind is also valued for its strong taste, ability to be dried and stored, and use in marmalades and perfumes. The élite of ancient Roman society enjoyed citrus fruits and increased their spread through Europe – which continued during the Middle Ages. Lemons were further spread through Europe by crusaders, but most medieval references to 'lemon' actually mean the aromatic citron. Dried citrus peels were a common European food ingredient. Later, both fruits and zest would be taken to the Americas by Spanish explorers.

SOURCES AND USES			
ORIGINS	**SPREAD**	**TASTE TYPE**	**CULINARY USES**
Southeast Asia – or Australia, New Caledonia and New Guinea	To northern Africa, then southern Europe Now in 140 countries, especially Spain and Italy, USA (particularly California, Arizona, Texas, Florida, Hawaii), Mexico, Brazil, China, South Africa and Australia	Sharp and bitter Floral aroma	Desserts, pastries, pies, puddings, sorbets Cakes, cookies, muffins Chocolate, lemon drops, candied orange peel Preserves, marmalade, pickles, chutney Bouquet garni, salads and as decoration Complements venison, duck, poultry Sweet and sour meals, curries Condiments, sauces, lemon pepper Liqueurs, cocktails, mulled wine

⏳ TRADITIONALLY USED FOR

Stomach cancer, kidney stones
Grapefruit zest lowers blood pressure
Citrus fruits' high vitamin C content prevents scurvy: British
    sailors were given citrus fruits on long voyages, hence the
    term 'limeys'

 ## MORE FOOD FACTS

Lemons have the highest concentration of the citrate salt.
The zest's essential oils are important flavourings and soften
    other strong flavours.
Candied peel (preserved in sugar) was popular in the
    1800s and is still used in cakes, breads and desserts.

 ## DID YOU KNOW?

The peel serves as a facial cleanser.
Lemons have been a primary commercial source of citric acid.
You can soak citrus zest in water, filter this and make a healthy
    drink.

MAKRUT LIME *Citrus hystrix*

It is best to refer to these limes as makrut rather than the alternative name kaffir as the latter is an offensive, illegal term in some cultures meaning variously a non-believer, non-Muslim or black African. The fragrant leaves of this wild lime tree join up to create a figure-of-eight, hour-glass loop. They add a distinctive citrus scent to many Thai and Southeast Asian meals, while the oil is used in perfumery. The thorny bush produces rough, lime-green fruit with bumps said to resemble the rough knobs over a crocodile's eyes. Its peel contains an essential oil similar to lime oil.

SOURCES AND USES			
ORIGINS	SPREAD	TASTE TYPE	CULINARY USES
Southeast and tropical Asia	Bangladesh, India, Indonesia, Malaysia, Nepal, the Philippines and Thailand	Spicy, lemony flavour Aromatic, astringent	In Indonesian, Lao, Cambodian, Creole, Vietnamese, Malaysian and Thai meals Soups and curries Chicken, fish, shrimps Vegetable noodle broth Rum Combines well with ginger, basil, chillies, garlic, coriander, coconut milk

 TRADITIONALLY USED FOR

Coughs, colds, sinus, chest congestion
Teas, tonics, indigestion treatments
Thai ointments and Malaysian tonics
As a shampoo to kill head lice
Keeping gums and teeth healthy
Hair and scalp cleansers
Purifying blood
Having a positive effect on the mind

 MORE FOOD FACTS

Leaves can be used like bay leaves – fresh, dried or frozen.
Substitute lemongrass if you can't find makrut.
The high-pectin seeds, tied in a muslin bag, help jams set.
In Cambodia, the entire fruit is crystallized and candied.
The sour fruit juice complements fish.

 DID YOU KNOW?

As well as a shampoo, it serves as bath essence, deodorant, air freshener and body spray.
Used in clothing detergents, it removes tough stains.
Lustral water mixed with makrut is used in Cambodian religious ceremonies.
Bruised leaves make a good hand wipe or potpourri ingredient.
Makrut is said to ward off evil spirits.

COCONUT *Cocos nucifera*

The name *coco* is Portuguese and means, variously, skull, head, grinning face, grimace, scarecrow, ghost, hobgoblin or witch – inspired by the coconut's face-like indentations. It was Vasco da Gama's shipmates who first brought the *coco* to Europe, and only when it came to England was the *'nut'* suffix added. Young coconuts contain a good quantity of sweet fluid and may be harvested for drinking. As well as this 'milk', these remarkably useful and versatile fruits provide food, oil, musical instruments, fuel, charcoal – and the husk fibre called coir which is great as a growing medium.

SOURCES AND USES			
ORIGINS	SPREAD	TASTE TYPE	CULINARY USES
Uncertain: either the Americas or Indo-Pacific Probably originated in South Pacific near what is now New Guinea	May have been carried by sea currents or be a Polynesian introduction Now grows in tropical coastal regions in more than 80 countries from as far north as Hawaii and as far south as Madagascar, including the Caribbean and Atlantic coasts of Africa and South America Top coconut-producing countries are the Philippines, Indonesia and India	Crunchy fibrous 'white flesh' Slightly sweet 'milk'	Oil for frying Solidified oil makes a kind of butter The flesh can be enjoyed fresh or dried (desiccated) Desserts, macaroons, chocolate bars Coconut milk is good in curries Coconut chips (in Hawaii and Caribbean) Palm sugar or jiggery, chutney Edible buds (palm cabbage) Coconut jam, candy, caramel and jelly Toddy, palm wine, arrack, coconut 'vodka'

 MORE FOOD FACTS

In Kerala's *puttu*, alternate layers of coconut and powdered rice are cooked in bamboo stalks.
Dried coconut flesh (copra) can be processed to produce coconut oil and meal.
Grated coconut flakes are used in coconut pie.

DID YOU KNOW?

Coconut water is sterile until the nut is opened and mixes easily with blood, so it was used during World War II for emergency transfusions and hydration.

Arabian Nights hero Sinbad the Sailor was said to have been a coconut dealer on his fifth voyage.

The coconut palm is called the Tree of Life but, botanically, is not really a tree since it has no bark or branches.

Legends claim that more deaths are caused by falling coconuts than by sharks.

One Australian octopus species uses coconut shells for defence and shelter.

In Thailand and Malaysia, trained pig-tailed macaques harvest coconuts.

It is the national tree in the Maldives and appears on their coat of arms.

 TRADITIONALLY USED FOR

Virgin coconut oil reduces cholesterol
Coconut peel may have anticancer attributes
Young coconut juice has estrogen-like characteristics
In Pakistan coconut is a traditional rat bite remedy
Tea from the husk fibre soothes inflammatory disorders
The roots treat diarrhoea and dysentery
Cups made from the shell are said to neutralize poisons in a drink
Smoke from burning shells and husks repels mosquitoes
The readily-absorbed oil is used in skin moisturizers, body butters, soaps, cosmetics, hair conditioners and massage oil

 OTHER USES

Coir is used to make doormats, brushes, sacks, string, rope, fishing nets, boat caulking, mattress and upholstery stuffing.

Coir makes a fine potting compost, especially for orchids.

Leaves are used to make mats, baskets, buckets, roofing thatch and, in India, to construct *pandal* sheds for marriage ceremonies.

The stiff mid-ribs of the leaves make brooms and arrows.

Shells are used to create bowls, ladles and buttons.

A dried half-coconut shell with husk will buff floors.

Half-coconut shells banged together imitate horse hoof beats in theatrical sound effects.

The trunk timber is straight, strong and salt-resistant so is an excellent material for bridges, houses, drums, containers and canoes.

Coconut oil makes a substitute for petroleum diesel.

Suits of armour with caps, back plates, leggings and jerkins were made in Micronesia out of densely woven coconut fibre matting.

STAR ANISE *Illicium verum*

Thriving in damp woodlands and alongside streams, this spice is named for its eight-pointed, star-like shape and anise taste – and for its lovely fragrance; the Latin name comes from *illicio* meaning 'entice'. The trees have glossy, evergreen leaves and yellowish green flowers tinged with pink or red, and are pollinated by insects, including beetles. Each seedpod 'petal' holds a single brown seed. The star-shaped fruits are fleshy when fresh, woody when dry, and best harvested just before ripening and then sun-dried to develop their aroma. It is widely used in Asian cooking and, being considerably less expensive to produce than aniseed (*Pimpinella anisum*), it has gradually displaced this in Western markets.

SOURCES AND USES			
ORIGINS	SPREAD	TASTE TYPE	CULINARY USES
Southwest China and Vietnam	Asian nations, especially China and India; New South Wales, Australia World production is now about 400 tonnes annually	Strong, mildly sweet, pungent, aromatic Fennel-like aroma with anise or liquorice notes	Chinese, Indian, Malay and Indonesian cuisines Asian spice mixes: Indian garam masala; main spice in Chinese five-spice mix Vietnamese beef and noodle Pho soup Enhances meat flavours With chicken, seafood, pork, root vegetables, pumpkin, tropical fruits and desserts Available as a tea Liqueurs: Galliano, sambuca, pastis, absinthe

  MORE FOOD FACTS

Star anise is sold as whole fruits, as fruit pieces or ground (best just before use).
The seeds contain a volatile aromatic oil.

 DID YOU KNOW?

A chemical in star anise is a major component of Tamiflu antiviral medication.
In Japan the tree is planted in temples and on tombs.
The powdered bark is used as incense.
The dried fruits are sweet-smelling and attractive in potpourri.
It scents soaps and perfumes.

TRADITIONALLY USED FOR

Chewing after meals to help digestion
Sweetening breath
A carminative, stimulant and diuretic
Colic, rheumatism and to warm bodies
Homoeopathic tinctures (from seeds)
To boost men's flagging libido

 WARNING

Beware of *Japanese star anise (Illicium anisatum)* as this is inedible and highly toxic.

 TRADITIONALLY USED FOR

Rheumatism, arthritis, bone and joint conditions
Flatulence, indigestion, heartburn
Chest complaints, bronchitis, tuberculosis
Cardiac and hepatic dropsy
Curing dropsy in sheep
Constipation, colic, gallstones
Childbirth, menstruation issues
Heart failure, gout, back pain
Urinary tract and prostate infections
Cancer, warts, gonorrhoea
Freshening bad breath
Bladder infections like cystitis

Fluid retention, high blood pressure
Skin conditions, inflammation, wounds
Asthma, colds, flu
A female contraceptive
It releases insulin from the pancreas, alleviating hunger in
    diet-controlled diabetics
Juniper tea was once used to disinfect surgeons' tools
Doctors often chewed the berries to prevent infection
Berries in the mouth were thought to help resist bubonic
    plague
Vets use the oil on animals' exposed wounds; it stops fly
    irritation

JUNIPER BERRIES *Juniperus communis* plus *J. drupacea, J. phoenicea, J. deppeana* and *J. californica*

Juniper is the only true spice derived from a conifer. This small shrub has green young berries and blue ripe ones, which are mentioned in an Egyptian papyrus from 1500 BCE and found in ancient Egyptian tombs, perhaps brought there from Greece. Greek athletes used the berries in Olympic events to improve physical stamina; for the Romans they served as an Indian pepper substitute. European folklore claims that if a juniper tree is planted by your door, no witch will enter. Its incense has been used in Scotland to ward off the evil eye and in Tibet to deter demons.

SOURCES AND USES			
ORIGINS	SPREAD	TASTE TYPE	CULINARY USES
Greece	Throughout northern hemisphere: Europe (particularly Scandinavia), North Africa, North Asia, North America (especially Texas and Oregon) Grown commercially in Hungary Grows abundantly in the Alps	Resinous, pine and citrus notes Mature dark berries usually preferred in cuisine Gin is flavoured with less mature green berries Combines well with black pepper, marjoram and laurel berries	Pepper substitute Adding a sharp, clear flavour to meat Complements wild birds like woodcock, game meat, boar, venison, pork With cabbage and sauerkraut In Alsatian, Norwegian, Swedish, German, Austrian, Czech, Polish and Hungarian dishes To make Swedish beer It flavours gin (and luncheon meats)

 MORE FOOD FACTS

The name gin comes from French *genièvre* or Dutch jenever, both meaning juniper.
Berries and branches are used in Finnish *sahti* beer.
Best used straight after harvesting but the berries are also available dried.
Juniper is particularly important in Alpine cuisines.

DID YOU KNOW?

In hot countries the tree yields a gum or varnish.
Juniper was the symbol of the Canaanites' fertility goddess, Ashera.
Native Americans used juniper as both food and appetite suppressant in times of hunger – and also made beads from the berries.
An essential oil extracted from juniper berries is used in aromatherapy and to make perfume.
Juniper cones are eaten by song birds and wild turkeys.

 WARNING Pregnant women and anyone with kidney weakness should use avoid over-use.

MULBERRY black, white and red *Morus nigra, M. alba* and *M. rubra*

Young mulberry fruits are white, green or pale yellow. In most species the ripening fruits turn pink then red, dark purple or black. The cultivation of white mulberry (whose berries remain white) to feed silkworms for China's vital silk industry began over 4,000 years ago; this variety can catapult pollen at 560 kilometres per hour (350 mph) – nearly half the speed of sound! All mulberry seeds are dispersed by birds who relish the fruit and then helpfully excrete the seeds elsewhere.

SOURCES AND USES			
ORIGINS	**SPREAD**	**TASTE TYPE**	**CULINARY USES**
Mesopotamia, Persia, China	Europe (especially Ukraine), Africa and America Afghanistan, Iraq, Iran, India, Pakistan, Syria, Turkey	Black and red are rich and very sweet White mulberries are bland	Fruit pastries, jams, sherbets The fruit is delicious fresh or dried Can be fermented into wine

 DID YOU KNOW?

In the 1600s, King James I imported 10,000 *black* mulberry trees to start an English silk weaving industry but silk worms feed only on the leaves of the *white* mulberry!

Now Buckingham Palace in London houses in its garden the National Collection of mulberries.

In German folklore, mulberry tree roots are used by the devil to polish his boots.

Mythological lovers Pyramus and Thisbe met their tragic deaths under a mulberry tree, staining the white fruits red with their blood. The gods then created the red mulberry to commemorate them.

It is said that English poet John Milton wrote *Paradise Lost* under a mulberry tree at Christ's College, Cambridge.

The nursery rhyme *Here we go round the mulberry bush* may have been composed by prisoners walking around the tree in Wakefield Prison's exercise yard.

 MORE FOOD FACTS

Dry mulberry wood is used for smoking meats.
English colonists in Virginia in 1607 noted the abundance of mulberry trees and how their fruit was eaten, sometimes boiled, by Powhatan tribes.

 TRADITIONALLY USED FOR

Improving the blood, stress
Prematurely grey hair
Constipation, diabetes, gout
Dental caries
Snakebites and haemorrhage
The bark, especially, is used to treat edema, promote urination, for coughs, wheezing, fever, food poisoning, headache, leukemia (still being researched) and sore eyes
The Romans used the leaves to treat mouth, trachea and lung diseases

PEPPER (BLACK AND WHITE) *Piper nigrum*

Pepper is a spreading, woody vine with small, white flowers on pendulous spikes. The fruit is called a drupe and then, when dried, a peppercorn. Black, green and white pepper are actually the same fruit, treated differently: black is the whole fruit picked half-ripe; white pepper is the seed removed from the darker-coloured skin, picked when very ripe; green peppercorns are unripe black ones, sometimes pickled. One of the most popular and most traded spices, it was known in Greece from at least the fourth century BCE. This 'king of spices' or 'black gold' has held such high prestige that it was used not only as a seasoning but also as currency, to pay taxes and ransoms, and as a sacred offering to honour the gods. Later, in the Middle Ages, the wealth of a man might be measured by his cherished pepper stockpile. It catalyzed much of the spice trade and led to the exploration of new lands and the development of major merchant cities in Europe and the Middle East.

SOURCES AND USES			
ORIGINS	SPREAD	TASTE TYPE	CULINARY USES
India, especially the Malabar Coast and Kerala	Southeast Asia: Thailand, Malaysia, Borneo, Cambodia, Vietnam Today's main exporters are Vietnam, India and Indonesia	Pungent, adds zest and heat Neither savoury nor sweet Either heat or milling releases the flavour	To enliven food and increase taste Soups, gravies, sauces Salads, vegetables, mashed potatoes, swede All meats, Chinese and Thai cuisine

MORE FOOD FACTS

The plants' flower spikes are spread out and sun-dried for several days (sometimes after blanching in hot water), then the peppercorns are stripped off the spikes.
Green peppercorns can be pickled in brine and vinegar.

TRADITIONALLY USED FOR

Indigestion and wind
Stimulating taste buds
Promoting sweating and urination
Stimulating breakdown of fat cells
Pepper oil is an ayurvedic massage oil, used in herbal treatments

DID YOU KNOW?

Pepper acts as an irritant inside the nose, stimulating nerve endings and making you sneeze.
When Rome declined in power, the invading Goths demanded a ransom of 3,000 pounds of pepper.
During the Middle Ages, peppercorns were accepted in lieu of money for dowries, rent and taxes.
Because pepper was used in lieu of currency, a 'peppercorn rent' means a token payment.
The vital pepper trade in Salem, Massachusetts, made some of America's first millionaires.
'Pepper' has long meant adding spirit or energy, hence the term 'pep up'.
A single stem will bear 20 to 30 fruiting spikes.
Black peppercorns were found stuffed in the nostrils of Egyptian Pharaoh Ramesses II.
Red and pink 'false pepper' is the seed of an entirely different South American tree, *Schinus molle*. Sichuan peppercorns also come from a different plant.

TAMARIND *Tamarindus indica*

The handsome tamarind produces fruit, timber for carpentry, and metal polish! Introduced to Mexico and South America in the 1500s by Iberian colonists, it has dense, bright green, drooping foliage and fragrant, red and yellow flowers. This 'date of India' produces delicious, highly-prized pods – not unlike runner beans but reddish-brown. Inside are small brown seeds, surrounded by a sticky, juicy pulp that, unusually for a fruit, contains calcium. Tamarind is sour, however, and it is said that Malabar pirates forced their captives to swallow a mixture of tamarind and seawater to make them regurgitate any hastily swallowed pearls.

SOURCES AND USES			
ORIGINS	**SPREAD**	**TASTE TYPE**	**CULINARY USES**
Tropical Africa	Tropical and subtropical China, Taiwan and Southeast Asia Arabia, India, Northern Australia Latin America, southern USA (Mexico and South Florida), West Indies India is largest producer	Sweet and sour Deliciously tangy High in tartaric acid and sugar	Fish, soups, curries, rice, prawns, meat, stews Sauce for duck and goose Pickles, chutneys, sweet and sour dishes Worcestershire and HP sauces Juices, soda drinks, iced fruit bars With pulses like lentils Desserts, jam, syrups, sorbets, ice creams

 ## MORE FOOD FACTS

Tamarind pulp has more sugar and acid per volume than any other fruit.
In Mexico, it is eaten raw and is also a snack – candied or dried and salted.
It can be rolled into balls with white sugar and spices.
Young tender leaves and flower buds serve as a vegetable.
A salad of tamarind leaves, boiled beans, crushed peanuts and fried onions is a Myanmar speciality.

 ## TRADITIONALLY USED FOR

Soothing fevers, sore throats, inflammation
Bowel problems, nausea, bile disorders
Indigestion, dysentery, worms
Sore eyes, conjunctivitis, ulcers
Boils, haemorrhoids, sunstroke
Rheumatism, swollen joints, sprains
Jaundice, asthma, diabetes, obesity
Anti-venom, malaria, wounds

DID YOU KNOW?

Geraniol, a phytochemical found in tamarind, may suppress pancreatic tumour growth.
Red tamarind wood is hard, dense and durable – ideal for furniture and floors.
Tamarind concentrate removes tarnish from brass and copper.
Infusing the leaves provides a yellow dye.
In India it is considered unsafe to sleep under the trees owing to the acid exhaled at night.
Tamarind makes an excellent bonsai tree.
Both fruits and leaves are adored by ring-tailed lemurs, which rely on the plant for up to 50 per cent of their diet in Madagascar.

VANILLA BEANS *Vanilla planifolio*

This is the second most valuable spice after saffron. Not only does the vanilla orchid of Central America require specific fungi for germination, but it blooms for just one single morning each year – and then only the Neotropical Melipona bee can pollinate it. The Spanish conquistador, Hernan Cortés, is said to have brought the plant to Europe in the 1520s, but Mexico still enjoyed sole production of vanilla for 300 years. Then, in 1841, a twelve-year-old slave boy on the island of Réunion discovered the trick of hand pollination, and this alternative, albeit laborious, solution put an end to Mexico's monopoly. Vanilla's name ultimately derives from the Latin *vagina* (sheath) and describes the shape of the long, black, wrinkled pods that contain thousands of tiny, black seeds. As the seed capsule ripens and dries, it crystallizes; the fruits glitter as if dusted with hoarfrost or diamond dust and then they release that delicious, sweet aroma.

SOURCES AND USES			
ORIGINS	SPREAD	TASTE TYPE	CULINARY USES
Mexico and Central America	Réunion, Mauritius and Comoros Islands Now throughout the tropics Indonesia and Madagascar are the world's largest producers	Pure, spicy, delicate A rare bouquet Flavours sweet dishes	Ice cream, custards, chocolate Caramel, syrups, coffee, cake

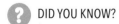

TRADITIONALLY USED FOR

Improving digestion, intestinal gas and fever
To flavour less palatable herbal medicines
An aphrodisiac
As an alternative to sugar, to reduce tooth decay

DID YOU KNOW?

Vanilla was cultivated and used as a flavouring by the Aztecs.
It was the French who developed vanilla ice cream.
Imitation vanilla now offers an affordable alternative.
The first vanilla orchid to flower in Europe was in London in
     1806; cuttings from this were sent to Holland and Paris
     but although the vines grew, they would not fruit without
     the Melipona bee.
Vanilla is also used in cigarettes and perfumes.
Scientists believe that it may help in the treatment of sickle
     cell disease.

BARK, TREES AND RESIN

FRANKINCENSE *Boswellia*

Frankincense is one of the three gifts the Wise Men presented to the infant Jesus in Bethlehem, signifying priestdom and holiness; it is mentioned in the Song of Solomon and was often mixed with oils to anoint newborn infants and initiates. In 1458 BCE in ancient Egypt, a mural in Queen Hatshepsut's temple depicted sacks of frankincense. It is tapped from trees (that sometimes grow out of solid rock) by slashing the bark; the resin bleeds out and hardens into 'tears'. Variations in trees, soils and climates produce slightly different resins. Frankincense was spread through Europe by crusaders, taken along the Incense Road and eventually reached China. Heavy raiding by nomadic Parthians ended the eastern trade after 300 CE.

SOURCES AND USES			
ORIGINS	**SPREAD**	**TASTE TYPE**	**CULINARY USES**
Arabia, Somaliland	Over 82 per cent comes from Somalia Some is grown in Southern Arabia Annual world production is *c.*200,000 tons	Warming, fragrant, like pine Subtle yet strong Balsamic, spicy, slightly lemony	Great with ice cream and shortbread Can be chewed as a gum but is stickier Try a drop or two of essential oil in honey

 MORE FOOD FACTS

Take in moderation only.
Should be translucent, with no dark impurities.

 TRADITIONALLY USED FOR

Incense, perfumes, aromatherapy
Promoting calm, serenity and relaxation
The oil relieves scorpion stings
A hemlock antidote
Vomiting, diarrhoea, digestion
Ulcers, tumours, colitis
Leprosy, fevers, depression, seizures
Arthritis, wounds, healthy skin, asthma
Female hormone system
Suppressing cancer cell viability
Bladder and ovarian cancer
A traditional medicine in Africa and Asia

DID YOU KNOW?

Frankincense purifies the air.
It relieves depression and anxiety in mice.
Some Egyptians warm their homes with incense braziers of frankincense.
Jews, Greeks and Romans also called it olibanum.
It was often transported in caravans or by elephant.
Arabs had to smoke out venomous snakes from the trees in order harvest the gum safely.
Ubar, a lost city in Oman now being excavated, may have been a frankincense trade centre.
Ancient Egyptian women used frankincense ash in their eye shadow.

CEYLON (TRUE) CINNAMON AND CASSIA
Cinnamomum verum or C. zeylanicum and C. cassia

Ceylon cinnamon and cassia (often sold as cinnamon in the USA) both derive from their trees' inner bark but Ceylon cinnamon is the finer quality. Cinnamon was being imported to Egypt by 2000 BCE and was ever highly prized – a gift fit for monarchs and gods, its source kept secret for centuries by spice trade suppliers. It was said to be guarded by winged serpents or fished up in nets at the edge of the world. In legends, both the phoenix and giant cinnamon birds built their nest from cinnamon and cassia sticks. In Roman times, the spice was sailed around the Arabian peninsular on rafts. Later, Indonesians transported it directly from the Moluccas to East Africa; local traders then carried it north to Alexandria (Egypt) from whence Venetian traders distributed the spice until Portuguese, Sinhalese and then Dutch traders seized the monopoly.

SOURCES AND USES			
ORIGINS	**SPREAD**	**TASTE TYPE**	**CULINARY USES**
True cinnamon: Arabia, Ethiopia, Sri Lanka, Bangladesh, India's Malabar coast Cassia: Southern China	Cinnamon: Myanmar, northern India, Brazil, Mauritius, Jamaica. In 1767, the East India Company established Asia's largest cinnamon estate in Kerala Cassia: Indonesia, Laos, Malaysia, Taiwan, Thailand, Vietnam, Sumatra, Ceylon, Japan, Java, Mexico and South America	True cinnamon: sweet, delicate, complex, crumbly texture, subtler and more aromatic Cassia: slightly darker, stronger, more pungent Oil is golden, hot, aromatic	Baking, pickling, marinades, teas, desserts, pastries, doughnuts, chicken, lamb, curries, making chocolate Greeks and Romans used it to flavour wine Spices cinnamon rolls and apple pie, fruits, coffee, tea, liqueurs, brandies Its distilled oil is used in a caraway sauce for oysters The buds also serve as a spice Used in Persian and Turkish cuisine for thick soups, drinks, sweets

 MORE FOOD FACTS

Ceylon cinnamon quills have many thin, easily powdered layers
Cassia sticks are much harder and denser, in a single layer
Cassia is a source of coumarin, a natural toxin; true cinnamon contains only traces

 DID YOU KNOW?

Cinnamon and cassia were gifted to the Miletus temple of Apollo.

Emperor Nero may have burned a year's worth of Rome's supply at his wife's funeral.

It was used in ancient Egypt as a beverage, flavouring, medicine and embalming agent and considered more precious than gold.

Cassia buds are like small cloves and have been enjoyed since the Middle Ages, especially in a spiced wine called Hippocras.

Moses was commanded to use both sweet cinnamon and cassia in holy anointing oil.

It was used for incense in Jerusalem's temples.

 TRADITIONALLY USED FOR

Unguents, potpourri, scenting garments

Diarrhoea, constipation, nausea, vomiting, flatulence

Womb haemorrhage, painful menstruation

Diabetes, digestion, reducing colon cancer risk

Boosting brain activity and memory

Lowering cholesterol, preventing heart disease

Warming cold or flu patients

A natural food preservative

Resisting fungus, bacteria, parasites, inflammation

 WARNING

Recent studies have revealed that regularly consuming cassia could result in potentially harmful levels of blood-thinning coumarin, damaging the liver and nervous system.

MYRRH *Commiphora molmol, C. abyssinica* and *C. myrrha*

This aromatic resin and natural gum is tapped from the bark of sturdy, thorny trees, often collected under the blazing sun in wild, rocky deserts. The gum quickly turns hard, glossy and a clear or opaque yellow that darkens, becoming streaked with white. It serves as perfume, holy ointment, incense and medicine and has been traded for 5,000 years, carried by camel caravans from Arabia to Petra and then sold throughout the Mediterranean. Egyptian Queen Hatshepsut sent an expedition to Africa to collect myrrh trees – as depicted in her temple. Thereafter, Egyptians used myrrh in embalming. In Syrian legend the tree is named for Thesis's daughter – transformed by the gods into a myrrh tree to escape her father's wrath.

SOURCES AND USES			
ORIGINS	**SPREAD**	**TASTE TYPE**	**CULINARY USES**
East Africa, Namibia, Southern Arabian Peninsula	Eastern Mediterranean, Ethiopia, Oman, Somalia	Bitter and spicy	Can be mixed with wine

 DID YOU KNOW?

Liquid myrrh is an ingredient of Jewish holy incense.
Myrrh was one of the gifts the Wise Men presented to Jesus.
A mixture of wine and myrrh was offered to Jesus during the crucifixion and used to anoint His body in the tomb.
Egyptians burned it to repel fleas.
It was offered to Roman prisoners before execution.
In the Bible (Esther 2:12) oil of myrrh was used to purify the new queen.
In olden times, the resin's sweet smoke lessened body odour.

 TRADITIONALLY USED FOR

Fever, ulcers,
Catarrh, laryngitis, colds, coughs, asthma, lung congestion
Ulcerated throat, gum disease, loose teeth, bad breath, toothache
Mouthwashes, gargles, toothpastes
Bruises, aches, sprains, painful swellings
Circulation, indigestion, appetite stimulation, diarrhoea
Heart, liver, spleen,
Rheumatism, arthritis
Wounds, bleeding
Menopause and uterine problems
Breast and lung cancer
To lower bad (and raise good) cholesterol
A broad-spectrum antiseptic preventing infection
Repelling mosquitoes and worms
Snakebites, hemlock poisoning
A healing salve in veterinary medicine
Leprosy, plague, scurvy
Baldness

DRAGON'S BLOOD *Daemomorops draco, Dracaena cinnabari* or *Dracaena draco*

This bright red resin comes from a range of species. From the rattan palm tree (*Daemomorops draco*) the red resin layer around unripe fruit is removed and rolled into solid balls. In other species, garnet-red drops are extracted from wounded trunks or branches. The Romans and Greeks also used the dragon tree *Dracaena cinnabari*, found on Socotra, an Indian Ocean island and important trading centre from the time of Ptolemaic Egypt on. Dragon's blood has been used since ancient times as incense, medicinal cure-all, dye, painting pigment and varnish. Many voodoo, hoodoo and folk traditions believe it offers power, protection, magic and good fortune. Medieval encyclopedias claimed it came from the blood of elephants and dragons that had died in mortal combat.

SOURCES AND USES			
ORIGINS	SPREAD	TASTE TYPE	CULINARY USES
Indonesia (*Daemomorops draco*) Canary Islands and Morocco (*Dracaena draco*) Socotra (*Dracaena cinnabari*)	Sumatra, Borneo, Southeast Asia	It tastes unpleasant but can be served with oatmeal and as an intoxicating drink	A syrup can be made from the roots The berries of the Socotra dragon tree are enjoyed by birds and domestic livestock

 ### DID YOU KNOW?

Adding dragon's blood to an incense or herb blend increases its potency.

It has been a source of varnish for furniture and Italian violins.

Dragon's blood was transported via the Incense Road.

It colours paper for banners and posters, especially for Chinese New Year.

It increases the potency of spells for protection, love, banishing and sexuality.

Although sold as 'red rock opium', it contains no opiates.

Giant *Dracaena draco* is one of the oldest living trees.

 ### TRADITIONALLY USED FOR

Diarrhoea, fever, dysentery, constipation, gastrointestinal problems

Acne, eczema

Tumours

Respiratory problems

Wound and lesion healing (is both coagulant and anticoagulant)

Mouth and throat ulcers

Chest pains, internal traumas, menstrual irregularities

Thaspine from *Croton lechleri* may be a useful cancer drug

Antiseptic, antiviral, antioxidant

 ### OTHER USES

Incense, aromatic smoke.
Spell-writing ink, ritual and medieval magic, alchemy.
Toothpaste, body oils, embalming.

Varnishes, plaster, photoengraving.
Decorating homes and pottery.
Colouring lipstick, dyeing wool.

ALLSPICE *Pimenta dioica*

Known by several other names such as Jamaica pepper, English pepper, myrtle pepper, pimenta, pimento, newspice, this evergreen can be a small scrubby shrub or grow into a tall canopy tree, often shading coffee trees below. The fruits are picked when green and unripe, then are dried in the sun until smooth and a reddish brown colour. The outer shell is the most important part. Christopher Columbus discovered the plant in Jamaica, and it was introduced into Europe during the 1500s. By 1621 the dried, unripe fruit had been dubbed 'allspice' by the English, who thought it tasted like a mixture of some of the sweeter spices. Repeated attempts at growing it in Europe from seeds failed and it was originally thought to thrive only in Jamaica, where it was spread by birds. In fact its origins were wider but passage through a bird's digestive system is essential for germination.

SOURCES AND USES			
ORIGINS	**SPREAD**	**TASTE TYPE**	**CULINARY USES**
Jamaica, Greater Antilles, Southern Mexico, Central America	Tonga, Hawaii Many tropical and subtropical zones	Like a mix of cinnamon, cloves, juniper and nutmeg Aromatic stimulant, not unlike strawberries when crushed	Desserts, pies, cakes Middle Eastern and Caribbean cuisine Jamaican jerk Pickling, curry powder Stews, casseroles, soups Cincinnati chilli Christmas pudding Pickled herring, sausages, puréed root vegetables Marinades, pâtés, terrines

 MORE FOOD FACTS

The leaves can be infused during cooking and then removed.
Indispensable in Middle Eastern cuisine.
A main element of barbecue sauce.
A West Indian allspice liqueur is named pimento dram.

 TRADITIONALLY USED FOR

Indigestion, flatulence
As an antimicrobial agent
Pimento Water in stomach and purgative medicines
Spice plasters: the berry extract is spread on linen to ease neuralgic or rheumatic pains

 DID YOU KNOW?

It is used as a deodorant and to scent soaps.
The oil is in cosmetics, including men's Old Spice products.
Caribbean Arawak people used it to cure meat.

The Latin name comes from the Portuguese *pimenta* (pepper) since the dried fruit looks like peppercorns.
Russian soldiers in the 1800s added allspice to their boots to keep their feet cosy.

SUMAC *Rhus*

Also spelt sumach, there are many varieties with greenish, creamy white or red flowers and crimson maple-like leaves that offer a glorious summer-end show (its name means 'red'). Bark, leaves, shoots and roots are all used while its red, brown and purple berries grind up into a deep-red or purple powder and act like salt, if applied generously. The milky fluid exuded from bark and leaves forms a solid gum that serves to make varnish, lacquer and dyes and to tan leather. American sumac tans leather yellow while European sumac helps create fine white leather for gloves and shoes.

SOURCES AND USES			
ORIGINS	SPREAD	TASTE TYPE	CULINARY USES
Africa, USA, Canada	Subtropical and temperate regions worldwide: the Americas, UK, Mediterranean, Middle East	Adds a salty, lemony taste to salads or meat Similar to tamarind but not bitter Hints of lavender	Good for low-salt diets Marinades, stuffing, meatballs, kebabs, stews Chicken, fish, seafood, salads Rice, legumes, breads In Indian lemonade (Rhus juice) and winemaking

 ## MORE FOOD FACTS

Wild sumac was used by Native Americans for food and medicine.
Young shoots and roots can be peeled and eaten raw.
The fruit can be eaten raw or cooked.
Mix with yogurt and herbs for delicious sauce or dip.
Use as a garnish on meze dishes like hummus.

 ## TRADITIONALLY USED FOR

Sore mouths and throats
Kidney and bladder problems, painful urination
Gonorrhoea, rectal bleeding, dysentery, diarrhoea
Colds, fevers, angina, diabetes, debility
Increasing breast milk
Burns, skin eruption, ulcers, scrofula

 ## OTHER USES

Root-bark is antiseptic, astringent, diuretic.
Leaf infusions help asthma.
Leaf poultices soothe rashes.
The leaves are chewed for sore gums and rubbed on sore lips.
Sumac berries treat diabetes, constipation, bed-wetting, quinsy, ringworm.
The blossoms make a soothing eye wash .
Its milky latex is a salve for sores and haemorrhoids.
Native Americans in Arizona, California and New Mexico use its wood to make baskets.
Leather tanned with sumac is light and flexible.
Beekeepers use dried sumac bobs as fuel for their smokers.
Sumac stems are used in Native American pipemaking.
Rhus oil can be made into candles.

 ## DID YOU KNOW?

The fruit of non-poisonous Rhus have crimson hairs; their panicles (a loose, branching cluster of flowers) are compound, dense, and terminal. Poison sumac and poison ivy have axillary panicles and smooth fruit, but today are not classified as sumacs.

SANDALWOOD *Santalum*

This is the world's second most expensive timber (after African Blackwood), for 4,000 years revered for its aroma, carving propensity and oil, used in perfumes, cosmetics, incense, aromatherapy and traditional medicine. Many an ancient temple and door is made from sandalwood, which retains its fragrance for decades and resists ant invasions. In 1792 the Sultan of Mysore decreed the trees royal so now in India and Pakistan these belong to the government, but many are illegally harvested. Sandalwood is made into rosaries, incense sticks, figurines, staffs and handcrafted ornaments. Rather than being felled, the trees are uprooted to allow the precious oil to be extracted from the roots.

SOURCES AND USES			
ORIGINS	SPREAD	TASTE TYPE	CULINARY USES
Indonesia and the Indian subcontinent	Nepal, Bangladesh, Sri Lanka, Pacific islands including Hawaii Western Australia is now a major exporter, especially of its oil	Distinctive, soft, warm, strongly aromatic Spicy and pungent	Australian Aboriginals eat the seed kernels, nuts and fruit There is a concentrated sandal drink Sandalwood powder mixed with honey, sugar and rice-water helps digestion Otherwise not generally used in cooking

 OTHER USES

Building, furniture-making, fuel.
Flavouring chewing tobacco.
Perfume, incense, soaps.
A fixative to floral and citrus fragrances.
An immersion oil within ultraviolet and fluorescence microscopy.
vIn India burning it on funeral pyres helped souls ascend to paradise and comforted mourners.
It has been used to make coffins for the wealthy.
In ceremonies the tree paste and its ash represent the element Earth.
It decorates deity icons.
The paste marks devotees' foreheads, indicating the Third Eye.
During meditation, its scent clears the mind, reduces desire and improves alertness.
Iranian Zoroastrian firekeeping priests maintain a permanent sandalwood fire.

 TRADITIONALLY USED FOR

Dry skin, dermatitis, psoriasis, prickly heat
Warts, itching, skin inflammation
Some skin cancers
Soothing stress and mental disturbance
Egyptian embalming
Traditional Chinese and Tibetan medicine, aromatherapy
Antibacterial; a urogenital and skin antiseptic
Bronchitis, gonorrhoea, cystitis
Mouthwashes and deodorants
Reducing fevers, headaches
Scorpion stings, snake bites

 DID YOU KNOW?

The stump has the highest oil content.
Sandalwood is a parasite: its roots penetrate host plants to obtain nutrients.
Its fragrance wards off evil spirits but attracts snakes.
In Hindu legends its trunk is covered by writhing serpents.

ROOTS, BULBS AND RHIZOMES

ONION *Allium*

Onions are a type of lily and may have been cultivated for over 5,000 years: they were a staple in prehistoric diets. Ancient Egyptians ate them at banquets and thought their spherical shape and concentric circles within circles symbolized eternal life, so included them in burial rites, believing their strong scent and magical powers might prompt the dead to breathe again. Pharaoh Ramesses IV (died 1160 BCE) was entombed with onions set into his eye sockets. In the Middle Ages, onions served as rent payments and wedding gifts. Their shape can be spherical or conical while colours range from white to golden brown, red and purple.

SOURCES AND USES			
ORIGINS	**SPREAD**	**TASTE TYPE**	**CULINARY USES**
West or Central Asia Possibly Iran and West Pakistan	Around the world Main producers: China (produces over 20 million tonnes annually), Egypt, India, USA	Sharp bouquet, pungent, bitter with a sweet note Odour ranges from mild to intolerable	Casseroles, soups, chutneys, pickles Thickens sauces, curries, gravies Making pastes with other spices To marinate meat or fish

 MORE FOOD FACTS

Can be baked, boiled, braised, eaten raw, fried, battered, grilled or roasted.
Rich in vitamin C.
When sliced, onions release chemicals which irritate the eyes, causing tears.

 DID YOU KNOW?

Athletes at the ancient Greek Olympics ate onions, drank the juice and rubbed their bodies with them to firm up muscles.
Pilgrims took onions to America but the Native Americans were already using them for food, clothing, dyes and toys.
Egyptian Pharaoh Cheops paid his pyramid builders in onions, garlic and parsley.
Around 9.2 million acres of onions are harvested annually.

 TRADITIONALLY USED FOR

Gravel, dropsy, hemorrhoids, dysentery, lumbago
Wounds, rashes, acne, boils, mouth sores
Reducing freckles
Bites by dogs, insects, snakes
Stimulating liver and bowel movements
Reducing colon cancer risk
Toothache, headaches, vision
Preventing high blood pressure, hair loss
Helping heart and nervous system
A sleep aid
Asthma and bronchitis
Helping erections and female fertility
An antiseptic, diuretic and appetite stimulant
A pest, moth and mole repellent
Onion syrup soothes coughs and colds
Roasted onions ease earache and tumours

 OTHER USES

Yellow-brown wool dyes.
Staining hard-boiled Easter eggs.
Polishing glass and copperware.
Preventing rust on iron.
Divination.

GARLIC *Allium sativum*

Used by humans for more than 7,000 years, garlic was celebrated in the days of the pyramids when the ancient Egyptians invoked garlic 'gods' if taking oaths. Wild, crow and field (or meadow) garlic are joined by the wild leek and elephant garlic from China, where it has been grown since 2000 BCE. Garlic is said to ward off vampires, werewolves, witches, monsters and demons, especially when worn, hung in windows and front doors (or shops in India), or rubbed on keyholes and chimneys. A Muslim legend claims that when Satan left the Garden of Eden, garlic sprang up below his left foot and onion under his right step.

SOURCES AND USES			
ORIGINS	SPREAD	TASTE TYPE	CULINARY USES
Uncertain: probably Siberia and Asia	Africa, Egypt, southern Europe, Sicily and then worldwide Widely grown in Latin Mediterranean nations and Provence Other garlic-growing areas include Egypt, Russia, South Korea and America Garlic is now grown in every USA state except Alaska China is today's greatest producer, with over 77 per cent of global output	Intensely aromatic, its spicy flavour sweetens with cooking Combines well with tomato, onion, ginger or yogurt	Flavours soups, stews, meat, vegetables, breads, oil, pasta, poultry, game Dumplings with pickled garlic are a favourite Chinese New Year dish

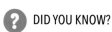 **DID YOU KNOW?**

Eating fresh parsley or taking a sauna may reduce garlicky breath.

Greek gladiators thought garlic gave them strength and courage.

Gilroy, California, calls itself the 'garlic capital of the world'.

Muslims who have eaten raw garlic are forbidden to pray in mosques.

Hungarian jockeys fastened garlic cloves to their horse bits so that any horses racing close behind would retreat from the scent.

Plague and fevers
Gunpowder injuries; stops wounds suppurating
Smallpox, dropsy
Parasites
Preventing colds
Poor digestion, low energy
Respiratory problems, pulmonary tuberculosis, asthma
Impotency
Sun-protection
Antibiotic, antiseptic and antifungal ointments

Deterring worms, birds, insects (including mosquitoes)
   and moles
Allixin (found in garlic) may help prevent cancer
Deterring vampires (allegedly)

 OTHER USES

Ancient Romans deemed garlic an aphrodisiac.

HORSERADISH *Armoracia rusticana* or *Cochlearia armoracia*

This brassica reaches 1.5 metres (4.9 feet) and, for 3,000 years, its white, tapered root has been appreciated – as noted by Egyptians, Greeks and Romans. In the Middle Ages both root and leaves were used in medicine. Later, USA presidents George Washington and Thomas Jefferson would mention it in their garden accounts. The word *horse* originally meant 'big, strong, and coarse'. English innkeepers grew the root to make cordials for exhausted travellers. In 1869, John Henry Heinz made horseradish sauce from one of his mother's recipes and bottled it in clear glass; it was one of the first American condiments and convenience foods.

SOURCES AND USES			
ORIGINS	**SPREAD**	**TASTE TYPE**	**CULINARY USES**
Russia and Ukraine, Southeastern Europe, Western Asia	Hungary, Germany, Poland, Finland, Denmark, UK	Distinctive, pungent, hot Once exposed to air or heat it loses its pungency	An accompaniment to roast beef, prime ribs, ham, oysters, hard-boiled eggs In soups, salads, mayonnaise, sandwich spreads Bloody Mary cocktails Its edible leaves are also eaten May enhance beef, chicken, seafood, red beet, fish, lamb, suckling pig, cheese and sausage

 MORE FOOD FACTS

Horseradish soup is an Easter Day speciality in Silesia, Poland.

The Japanese condiment, wasabi, may be made with horseradish.

Germans still brew horseradish schnapps; some add it to their beer.

In Southern Germany horseradish 'Kren' is traditionally served with beef and lingonberries at weddings.

It may be one of the five bitter herbs in the Jewish Passover Feast.

 TRADITIONALLY USED FOR

A stimulant, diuretic, antiseptic, digestive aid

Stimulating perspiration

Dropsy, scurvy, chilblains

Sciatica, gout, joint-ache, rheumatism

Spleen and liver swellings

An aphrodisiac

Improving skin, removing freckles

Common cold, coughs, hoarseness, whooping-cough, tuberculosis

Backache and pains, neuralgia, menstrual cramps, headaches

Expelling worms

 DID YOU KNOW?

Horseradish poisons horses.

It was depicted on a mural in the Roman city of Pompeii.

The Delphi Oracle announced that horseradish was worth its weight in gold.

Horseradish was called 'stingnose' in some parts of the USA.

The Guinness Book of World Records notes that Al Weider tossed a horseradish root over 24 metres (80.5 feet).

ARROWROOT *Maranta arundinacea*

Arrowroot, very popular in the 1800s, may have been cultivated for 7,000 years. Its name was inspired by how Caribbean people used this semi-tropical plant to treat poisoned arrow wounds – it draws out toxins from injuries. It was also known as the obedience plant. It has hairy, spiky leaves, clusters of creamy white flowers and roots full of a starch powder that, once extracted, creaks and crackles like fresh snow. Its starch served to wean infants and nourish patients with digestive difficulties. It was a major export from St Vincent from 1900 to 1965, when it played a vital role in the island's economy, contributing some 50 per cent of foreign export earnings.

SOURCES AND USES			
ORIGINS	SPREAD	TASTE TYPE	CULINARY USES
West Indies (St Vincent, Jamaica, Bermuda, Guyana) Georgia, North America Western Brazil Possibly Central America	Central India, Bengal, Southeast Asia, Australia, South and West Africa, Philippines, Mauritius	An odour like French beans	For thickening, like corn starch Juices, syrups Hot sauces, clear sweet and sour (and fruit) sauces Seasoning (with sugar and nutmeg) Arrowroot biscuits and cakes Mix with milk and animal jelly Pudding, blancmange, jellies Roots can be candied Beef tea, veal broth Korean and Vietnamese noodles Instead of wheat flour in baking (but not in bread)

 ## MORE FOOD FACTS

It prevents ice crystals forming in homemade ice cream.
When heated the starch turns to jelly.
Arrowroot is a powdery, highly digestible starch.
In Burma, arrowroot tubers are boiled (or steamed) and
    eaten with salt and oil.

 ## TRADITIONALLY USED FOR

Convalescent patients
Bowel complaints
Gangrene
Wounds
Scorpion and black spider bites
Vegetable poisons like savanna (camel poison) tree

 ## DID YOU KNOW?

Slaves in the West Indies processed arrowroot and, once
    freed, many then grew their own.
As the American Civil War began, the American magazine
    Godey's Lady's Book included a primer on arrowroot
    cookery.

 ## OTHER USES

The starch is a good substitute for talcum powder.
Paper-making.

TURMERIC *Curcuma longa*

Used in Asia for thousands of years, this rhizome is a member of the ginger family that thrives in warm, wet conditions and grows wild in the forest. The plants form well-branched, yellow to orange, aromatic rhizomes that are gathered annually and used fresh or – once boiled and dried – ground into a deep, orange-yellow powder that adds colour and warmth to Indian cuisine and many a curry. It has a very long history of medicinal use, dating back nearly 4,000 years to the Vedic culture in India, where it was a culinary spice and often present in religious ceremonies (as it is still today). In 1280, Marco Polo described this spice and its similarities to saffron.

SOURCES AND USES			
ORIGINS	SPREAD	TASTE TYPE	CULINARY USES
Southeast India	South Asia including China, Indonesia, Nepal, the Philippines, Taiwan Jamaica, Haiti, West Africa	Earthy, slightly bitter Warm and peppery Mustard odour	South Asian and Middle Eastern cooking; vegetable and meat dishes Curries Some desserts and pickles Iranian and Thai recipes Vietnamese stir-fries and soups Its golden colour augments mustards, boiled rice, canned drinks, cakes, biscuits, ice cream, yogurt, orange juice, popcorn, cereals, sauces, cheeses, butter, margarine, salad dressings, chicken soup

 ## MORE FOOD FACTS

If not for immediate use, the rhizomes are boiled and then dried in a hot oven.

The leaves are used to wrap and cook food (Goans layer rice flour and coconut cane sugar on the leaves; then close and steam these).

 ## OTHER USES

Its orange-yellow dye colours fabric, temporary tattoos, Easter eggs, playdough.

Turmeric paper is used to test for acidity or alkalinity.

It is a thanksgiving offering to the sun god during Indian harvest festivals.

In India, tubers may be used as marriage necklaces or be tied to the couple's wrists.

 ## TRADITIONALLY USED FOR

Traditional Indian (Siddha) and Chinese medicine

Stomach and liver ailments, jaundice, abdominal pain

Reducing gas, colic, bloating

Cleansing and healing wounds, sores, cuts, burns

Irritable bowel syndrome, dissolving gallstones

Blood in urine, menstrual problems, haemorrhaging

Toothache, whitening teeth

Aches, sprains, bruises, joint pain, arthritis

Eczema, allergies, scabies, chicken pox, shingles, psoriasis, acne

Colds, sore throats, runny noses, coughs, sinusitis

Dandruff, swimmer's ear, protecting the heart, anorexia

Resisting viruses, microbes and bacteria

Its active compounds may be anti-inflammatory, antitumour, antioxidant, antifungal and it is a potential treatment for diabetes, lowering cholesterol counts, Alzheimer's disease, childhood leukemia, melanoma and cancers of the breast, colon, prostate and lung

❓ DID YOU KNOW?

In medieval times, it was an alternative to expensive saffron and called Indian saffron in Europe.

The name 'turmeric' derives from an Iranian word for saffron.

The robes of Hindu monks were dyed yellow with turmeric.

It is used in sunscreens, face creams, soap and body scrubs.

The paste is applied by some women in India to remove superfluous hair.

Turmeric paste is used on the skin of brides and grooms before marriage in some parts of India, Bangladesh and Pakistan to make the skin glow and to deter bacteria.

Because of its yellow-orange colouring, turmeric was associated with the sun.

Drinking turmeric tea may increase longevity.

Susruta's Ayurvedic *Compendium* (250 BCE) suggests a turmeric ointment to relieve poisoning.

△ WARNING

It is unsafe during pregnancy, can exacerbate gallbladder problems and slows blood clotting.

LIQUORICE *Glycrrhiza glabra*

This tall, late-blossoming plant has purple and white flowers, maroon seedpods and a long taproot prized for its rich flavor for over 3,000 years: it was enjoyed by Egypt's Pharaoh Tutankhamun, ancient Chinese and Greeks, Alexander the Great, Roman Emperor Caesar and Native Americans. Roman soldiers carried liquorice (also spelt licorice) with them as they marched north through Europe. It was brought to England by Dominican friars; the flat liquorice tablets called Pontefract cakes were created at Pontefract Abbey in Yorkshire where an annual Liquorice Festival is still held today – a liquorice queen wearing liquorice clothes and jewellery is crowned with a liquorice crown, watched by visitors enjoying liquorice cheese!

SOURCES AND USES			
ORIGINS	**SPREAD**	**TASTE TYPE**	**CULINARY USES**
Asia, Africa	Southern Europe, North America, Australia India, Iran, Afghanistan, China, Pakistan, Iraq, Azerbaijan, Uzbekistan, Turkmenistan, Turkey Spain is the largest producer	Its sweet constituent, glycyrrhizin, is 40 times sweeter than sugar, tarter and less immediate but longer lasting Bitter and intense	Confectionary, soft drinks, tea, brewing, aperitifs, liqueurs May be sold liquid, dry, powdered or peeled

 MORE FOOD FACTS

In sweets and candies, it may be mixed with aniseed, mint, menthol or laurel.
It is beloved in Italy.
It is a popular liqueur in Calabria and a drink in Syria.
Saltly liquorice is enjoyed in Scandinavia.

 OTHER USES

To prevent baldness and dandruff.
Tobacco flavouring.
It can be chewed as a mouth freshener.
Brewers used it to add colour and flavour; its root enzymes stabilize the beer's foam head.

 DID YOU KNOW?

In the 1930s the root was sold in America's 10-cent stores.
The shoe eaten by Charlie Chaplin in *The Tramp* was made
    of liquorice.
During the Second World War British and Japanese soldiers
    in the jungle were given liquorice to quench their thirst.
Hannibal fed it to his elephants to help them carry his army
    across the Alps.
Egyptian pharaohs used it in *erqesos*, a traditional healing
    tonic drink.
It may be called 'Spanish' in northern England where
    Spanish monks grew it at Rievaulx Abbey.

 TRADITIONALLY USED FOR

Raising blood pressure
Rejuvenation (slows brain-aging)
Respiratory problems, dry coughs, asthma, colds, flu, sore
    throat, emphysema
As a flavouring, making medicine palatable
Dermatitis, tooth decay, gingivitis
Chronic fatigue, depression, stress
Athlete's foot, fungal infections, psoriasis, canker sores,
    ulcers, yeast infections
Body odour
Gout, arthritis
Heartburn, liver problems, prostate enlargement,
    menopause
HIV, Lyme disease, tuberculosis, shingles, tendinitis
Antiviral, antimicrobial, anti-inflammatory, antitumour
Liquorice root is used in modern Chinese cancer
    treatments

ORRIS ROOT *Iris Germanica* and *I. pallida*

Orris is the root of the majestic iris that thrives on the fringe of rivers and lakes, or flaunts its brilliant rainbow colours in meadows and rocky areas. A fresco in King Minos's palace in Crete, dating to about 2100 BCE, includes elegant irises while ancient Egyptians placed them on their royal sceptres and the Sphinx's brow – its three petals signifying faith, wisdom and valour. In Greek mythology, Iris carried messages from Heaven to Earth, using the rainbows as her pathway. She led young girls into the afterlife and so represented lost love and grief; Greek men would plant an iris on the grave of a lost loved one. Orris root, mixed with anise, was used to scent linen in medieval times and has long been the source of delicate violet-like perfumes.

SOURCES AND USES			
ORIGINS	**SPREAD**	**TASTE TYPE**	**CULINARY USES**
Southern Europe, especially Italy	Morocco Florence is still an orris root production and perfume-making centre	Like raspberry and violet; woody	To give a unique flavour to gins and brandies To make raspberry-like syrups and flavourings To flavour a Russian honey and ginger drink Orris root is an ingredient of *Ras el hanout*, a Middle Eastern and North African herb and spice blend, especially popular in Morocco

 TRADITIONALLY USED FOR

Lungs, coughs, hoarseness
Liver, pancreas, kidneys, goitre, syphilis
Gastric pain, diarrhoea
Chronic jaundice, psoriasis, eczema, open ulcers, skin infections
Migraine, nausea, vomiting, 'morning sickness'
Earache
Bad breath, removing freckles
The juice of fresh roots, bruised with wine, treat dropsy
As a paste to treat wounds and ulcers

 OTHER USES

To flavour toothpastes and cachous.
As a snuff.
A perfume fixative.
To make rosary beads and teething rings.
In ancient Rome, chalk and orris root formed make-up foundations.
Powdered orris root scents linen, pomander balls, spice wreaths and potpourri.

DID YOU KNOW?

The powder is blown onto clothes and sheets to make sure that the owner returns one's love.
Queen Elizabeth I of England wore a gown embroidered with iris blooms.

GINSENG *Panax ginseng and P. quinquefolius*

Recommended some 5,000 years ago in the Indian Vedas, ginseng was believed to provide the lusty strength of the bull, horse, mule, goat and ram and to make men breathe fire! The Chinese have used it for thousands of years, believing that it increases energy and enhances sexual performance, possibly inspired by the root's parsnip-like branched shape that forks as it matures and resembles a man's legs. The five-lobed, hand-shaped Ginseng leaf, albeit not so highly prized, is also used. The root was worth more than gold during China's Qing Dynasty and is still expensive. Difficult to cultivate and taking a good six years to mature, it is called the magical herb, divine root, bloodlike, five fingers, red berry, root of life and the kingly herb. Native Americans also knew of its powers.

SOURCES AND USES			
ORIGINS	SPREAD	TASTE TYPE	CULINARY USES
Manchuria Mountains, China North America	Korea (historically, the largest provider, with China the greatest consumer) Eastern Asia, northeast China, Bhutan, eastern Siberia and Vietnam Eastern and central North America	Aromatic	The whitish root turns red and hard once steamed and dried White ginseng, native to America, is dried without being heated Used in herbal teas, ginseng coffee and energy drinks

 DID YOU KNOW?

Its Greek name *panax* means 'all-heal', like Panacea, the Greek goddess of universal remedy.

Red ginseng is more stimulating than the white form.

Wild ginseng is relatively rare and increasingly endangered.

In 221 BCE 3,000 foot soldiers were sent by the Chinese emperor to find wild ginseng; those who returned empty-handed were beheaded.

In Korea, ginseng gatherers purified themselves for a week; they needed to be clean and chaste to see the ginseng leaves that glowed in the moonlight.

Only gatherers who were of pure heart were able to find ginseng. Hunters risked their lives as panthers and tigers also sought the root.

The Chinese White Swans bandits attacked gatherers (who were armed only with a stick) and stole their finds, or tortured them to discover the ginseng location. They then gave their victims a red flag to carry in order not to be attacked again

Hunters would pray to the spirit of the panther, the tiger and the mountain. The legendary spirit inside the root would lead those who were evil deep into the forest to be lost forever.

TRADITIONALLY USED FOR

An aphrodisiac, improving sexual drive

Easing stress and calming body

Slowing aging, preventing disease

Relaxing muscles

Diabetes type 2

Mental and bodily fatigue

Pulmonary complaints

Tumours

Fevers, headaches

North Americans had long considered it to be one of their most sacred herbs and used it to soothe eyes, as a wound poultice and to cure headaches and croup

 OTHER USES

Hair tonics and cosmetics.

GINGER *Zingiber officinale*

Ginger root creeps underground and in spring sends up its stalk topped by a scalloped spike supporting clusters of white and pink buds that become white or yellow flowers. Crusaders and pilgrims returning from the Holy Land introduced ginger to Europe and it was soon a vital part of the spice trade. Jamaican ginger was the first oriental spice grown in the Americas and imported back to Europe. In the 1500s, Francisco de Mendosa transplanted it from the East Indies into Spain. Lavish gingerbread houses, inspired by the *Hansel and Gretel* story, became popular in the 1800s. As William Shakespeare wrote in *Love's Labour's Lost*: 'An I had but one penny in the world, thou should'st have it to buy ginger-bread.'

SOURCES AND USES			
ORIGINS	SPREAD	TASTE TYPE	CULINARY USES
Southern China	Northern China, Indonesia (Spice Islands), India, Nepal and Thailand Caribbean, West Africa – especially Nigeria Main producers: India and Jamaica	Hot, fragrant, aromatic, biting, pungent	With vegetables; in gravies, sauces, soups To spice coffee and tea To make ginger tea, often with honey Ginger wine – made commercially since 1740 Ginger beer, ale and liqueurs To flavour Asian dishes of seafood, meats, fish, tofu and noodles Gingerbread, cakes, cookies, biscuits, candies, crackers, ginger snaps Candied or crystallized ginger

 OTHER USES

It is used to disguise the taste of medicines.
In Chinese medicine ginger is a 'yang' tonic; it boosts energy, body temperature and vitality.

 TRADITIONALLY USED FOR

Slowing or preventing tumour growth
Nausea, vomiting, sea/morning sickness
Gastritis, diarrhoea, constipation, colic
Colds, flu prevention, coughs, sore throats
Arthritis, joint/muscle injury, rheumatism
Headaches, fatigue, stomachache
Cleansing the body through perspiration

 WARNING

Some studies advise against taking ginger during pregnancy.

 MORE FOOD FACTS

Compliments chicken and meat dishes with onion and garlic.

As a salad – try shredded raw ginger with nuts and seeds.

Ginger garlic paste adds warmth and spice.

Try adding fresh finely chopped leaves to shrimp soup.

Preserved ginger is made by steeping the root in hot syrup.

Lime and lemon complement ginger well.

Ginger beer was imported to Greece by the British Army and became a Corfu favourite called Tsitsibíra.

Whisky Mac is a cocktail made from whisky and ginger wine.

 DID YOU KNOW?

Its name comes from a Sanskrit word for 'horn root', after ginger's knobbly shape.

The Greeks wrapped bread around ginger and ate it to ease indigestion – hence gingerbread.

Chinese sailors chewed on the root to combat seasickness.

In 992 the Armenian monk Gregory Nicopolis created modern gingerbread, showing French priests how to make the sweet dough.

Medieval ladies presented gingerbread cakes to their favourite knights.

England's Queen Elizabeth I devised the gingerbread man, offering it to foreign diplomats.

In the 1800s, people believed ginger wine prevented cholera.

Ginger is used in electronic cigarettes.

Rich Europeans used as much table ginger as salt in the 1800s.

OTHER SOURCES

ANGELICA *Angelica archangelica* or *Archangelica officinalis*

Also called Norwegian angelica, Holy Ghost and archangel, angelica thrives in colder climates, even subarctic regions, enjoying damp spots on moors, pastures, mountain and coastal regions, stream-and riversides. It can reach as high as three metres (nearly ten feet), with white or greenish-white sparkling pomanders of flowers pollinated by many insects including bees and moths. Tales tell that in the fourteenth century angelica was revealed to physician Mattheus Sylvaticus by an archangel – hence its name and reputed angelic, plague-curing virtues! It is also said to bloom on the saint day of Michael the Archangel. Its ridged stems may have inspired the fluted Doric columns of ancient Greek architecture.

SOURCES AND USES			
ORIGINS	**SPREAD**	**TASTE TYPE**	**CULINARY USES**
It may have Nordic origins or come from Syria or Africa	Northern hemisphere up to Iceland and Lapland Northern Russia, Lithuania, Norway Southeast Asia	Pleasantly aromatic Even the roots are fragrant	Crystallized stem strips make tasty cake decorations Roots and seeds flavour gin plus Vermouth and Chartreuse liqueurs Seacoast angelica is eaten like wild celery Dried aromatic leaves are used in hop bitters The fresh herb flavours boiled or steamed fish

 MORE FOOD FACTS

Roots, seeds and leaves are all used.
Icelanders eat both stem and roots raw, with butter.
Finns eat the young stems baked in hot ashes.
Norwegians make bread with the roots.
Japanese deep-fry battered angelica tempura.

 DID YOU KNOW?

It flourishes in London's Lincoln's Inn Fields and was common by the Tower of London.
Laplanders use the roots as food and the stalks to make medicine and reed musical instruments.

 TRADITIONALLY USED FOR

Resisting plague
Colds and respiratory ailments, chronic bronchitis, all lung and chest diseases
Healing wounds
Purifying blood: a remedy for fevers, poisons, agues and all infectious maladies
Flatulence, rheumatism, gout
Mad-dog bites and venomous stings

 OTHER USES

Angelica baths remove curses and make purification spells.
Slices of the hollow stalk act as earwig traps.
Several North American First Nations used angelica in their rituals.

WORMWOOD *Artemisia absinthium*

Wormwood is the bitterest of herbs and thrives on shaded arid ground, dry plains, rocky slopes, steppes and at the edge of footpaths and fields. Both the whole herb and its aromatic leaves are used as a spice. Its straight, tall stems are silvery-green, bearing greenish-grey leaves (which have tiny oil-producing glands) and pale yellow, tubular flowers. The genus is named after Artemis, the Greek name for the goddess and huntress, Diana. Wormwood is a major ingredient in absinthe, an anise-flavoured spirit associated with the death of author Edgar Allan Poe and the suicide of Dutch artist Vincent van Gogh.

SOURCES AND USES			
ORIGINS	SPREAD	TASTE TYPE	CULINARY USES
Asia and Europe	North America, Eurasia, northern Africa	Intensely bitter, pungent, warm	Flavouring spirits and wines, herbal bitters, absinthe and Pelinkovac liqueur Sometimes used instead of hops in beer

 ## DID YOU KNOW?

'Bitter as Wormwood' is an ancient saying.
It was strewn among clothes and furs to deter moths and insects.
L'Absinthe is an Edgar Degas painting showing the effects of intoxication.
In the Bible, wormwood represents an injustice, calamity or curse.

 ## OTHER USES

To repel and kill insects.
Its essential oil expels tapeworms, threadworms and roundworms from humans, dogs and cats.
Names include:
Absinthe
Common wormwood, warmot, southernwood
Girdle of St John, holy seed
Old man, Old woman, Lad's love
Green ginger
Mingwort

 ## TRADITIONALLY USED FOR

Jaundice, dropsy, ague, fever
Parasites, sclerosis, skin irritation
Anxiety, melancholy, nerves, depression, irritability
Anaemia, liver problems (including cancer)
Childbirth pain
Debility, tremors
Heartburn, indigestion, poor appetite, flatulence, gastric issues
Migraine
Gout, rheumatism
Leukemia
Wounds
Antiseptic fomentations

 ## MORE FOOD FACTS

Leaves and flowering tops are used.
In the Middle Ages, it spiced mead.
It can flavour vermouth.

 WARNING
The US Food and Drug Administration classifies wormwood as unsafe.
Ingesting large amounts can cause kidney failure and convulsions.

CAPER BUSH or FLINDERS ROSE *Capparis spinosa*

The Flinders rose, with its round, fleshy leaves and pinkish-white flowers, revels in strong sunlight and a long growing period. It is the edible, dark-olive-green buds or capers that are used as a seasoning; the fruits (caper berries) are generally eaten pickled and the leaves are enjoyed in salads. The caper bush thrives on rocky Himalayan slopes, Pakistan's sand dunes, Adriatic escarpments, in dry coastal regions of Egypt, Libya and Tunisia, in transitional zones between salt marsh and coastal desert on the Asian Red Sea coast, in the rocky Jordan valley, on Israel's sandstone cliffs and Australia's coastal dunes. It clings to crevices and cracks on many an ancient Roman fortress wall!

SOURCES AND USES			
ORIGINS	SPREAD	TASTE TYPE	CULINARY USES
Western, Central and Southwest Asia and the tropics	Mediterranean basin, East Africa, Morocco, Iberian peninsula, Turkey, Italian islands, Madagascar, Himalayas, Pacific islands and Australia	Spicy, a little sour, slightly astringent, pungent Mustard oil is released from the bud to create an intense flavour	Capers are an ingredient of Tartare sauce and Greek *mezze* Capers season or garnish salads, pasta, meat dishes, sauces, chicken, fish and spaghetti dishes, soups They go well served with smoked salmon and cream cheese Caper berries are eaten pickled Use the leaves in salads Young shoots can be cooked and served like asparagus

 MORE FOOD FACTS

Used in Mediterranean cuisine, especially in Southern Italy and Sicily, Cyprus and Malta.
Capers and caper berries can garnish Martini drinks.
Pickled caper berries are a popular Menorcan snack.
Dried caper leaves serve as a rennet substitute in cheese-making.

 DID YOU KNOW?

Unripe nasturtium seeds can be substituted for capers.
In Biblical times, the caper berry was said to be an aphrodisiac.

 TRADITIONALLY USED FOR

Gas and flatulence, diarrhoea
Gout, rheumatism, aching joints
Viral hepatitis and liver cirrhosis
Skin conditions, bruising
Coughs
Eye infections, cataracts
Stomach pain, vaginal thrush
Cancer prevention
Anti-inflammatory, antiviral and antioxidant
Herbal teas made of caper root and young shoots soothe rheumatism
Sprouts, roots, leaves and seeds reduce inflammation

⭐ **OTHER USES**

Disguising rashes, wrinkles and capillary weaknesses.

SAFFRON *Crocus sativus*

In autumn, each saffron crocus bears up to four lilac or mauve flowers with a sweet, honey-like fragrance. Each bloom flaunts three bright crimson stigmas – and it is these that are used as both seasoning and a colouring agent to give food and textiles a brilliant golden hue. Today saffron is one of the world's most costly spices but it was known in late Bronze Age Crete and an Assyrian botanical from the seventh century BCE indicates that it has been traded across four millennia. The stigmas were traditionally picked at dawn – before the flowers opened, in order to retain the aroma. In some areas only innocent young girls were allowed to pick saffron. Today it is more often elderly women who undertake the arduous handpicking of the delicate stigmas. A main ingredient of magic potions in ancient times, saffron used to be sprinkled between sheets and might be brewed in tea to make a man fall in love or to dispel melancholy. In medieval times, anyone daring to adulterate saffron with cheaper ingredients was likely to be burnt alive.

SOURCES AND USES			
ORIGINS	**SPREAD**	**TASTE TYPE**	**CULINARY USES**
Southwest Asia and Greece (Crete)	Spain, North Africa, North America, Oceania Iran accounts for 90 per cent of the world's harvest	Semi-sweet, slightly bitter, faint honey flavour Like hay or grass and seaside iodine	Rice, risotto, paella, seafood, soups, French bouillabaisse Kashmiri lamb Arabic coffee may include saffron and cardamom

 TRADITIONALLY USED FOR

Antibacterial and antiviral properties
Stomachache, flatulence, heartburn
Menstrual cramps
Premature ejaculation
Cancer, Alzheimer's disease
Coughs, asthma, bronchitis, loosening phlegm
Baldness, dry skin
Depression, shock, insomnia
Soothing measles (saffron 'tea' with brandy)

 MORE FOOD FACTS

Wines and many liqueurs, as well as vodka and gin, may be aromatized with saffron.
For best results, infuse saffron in warm water, milk or stock for 20 minutes to draw out colour and flavour; then add liquid to dish.

DID YOU KNOW?

In its near 4,000 years of use, saffron has treated at least 90 different ailments.

It can take 75,000 saffron blossoms to produce 1 pound of saffron spice.

Alexander the Great used Persian saffron in his infusions, rice, and baths to cure his battle wounds.

Saffron has specialist tasters, who decide which varieties are best.

The aroma on the skin after a hot saffron bath is said to drive lovers wild with desire.

The name saffron derives from Arabic *za'feran* and *da asfar*, meaning yellow.

In ancient India, robes were traditionally dyed golden yellow with a saffron dye and Buddhist priests made this the official color of their robes, albeit usually dyed with cheaper turmeric or jackfruit.

Saffron was used as a perfume and cosmetic by Greek courtesans and Egyptian queen Cleopatra.

Demand for saffron rose during the fourteenth-century Black Death: Europe imported large quantities via Venetian and Genoan ships and the seizure of one shipment sparked the Saffron War.

⭐ OTHER USES

A cosmetic in ancient times.

Its yellow dye is used on fabric and leather.

Fragrance in perfume.

A hangover cure: Romans slept on saffron-stuffed pillows.

LEMONGRASS *Cymbopogon citratus*

A member of the sugar cane family, lemongrass creates a graceful fountain of ornamental grass. It has many other names, including silky heads, barbed wire grass, citronella grass, fever grass and sweet rush (because of its speedy release of tension). It is used to make citronella oil for soaps, candles and insect repellants (especially effective against mosquitoes). It helps to preserve ancient Indian palm-leaf manuscripts as its oil injects a natural flexibility into the brittle leaves, keeps the manuscripts dry and deters any insect invasion.

SOURCES AND USES			
ORIGINS	**SPREAD**	**TASTE TYPE**	**CULINARY USES**
Nepal Sri Lanka and South India Indonesia	India and Southeast Asia Oceania USA (especially California and Florida) Most warm temperate and tropical regions	Subtle, sweet citrus/ ginger	Essential in Thai, Vietnamese and Indochinese cuisine Teas, noodle soups, stews, curries Compliments poultry, fish, beef, seafood Good with steamed shellfish like mussels and clams Add to coconut milk for braising beef or pork Tender bruised and braised stalks can infuse spirits or cocktails

 ## MORE FOOD FACTS

Can be used fresh or dried and powdered.
Add to lemonade or sorbets.
It is drunk as a tea in African and Latin American countries.
It masks too-strong or 'gamey' scents.

 ## DID YOU KNOW?

Lemongrass oil is similar to the pheromone created by the honeybee and so can serve to lure a fresh swarm or to draw the attention of hived bees.
It deters insects and helps some vegetables (like tomatoes and broccoli) to thrive unmolested.

 ## TRADITIONALLY USED FOR

Detoxifying: it stimulates kidney, liver, pancreas and bladder
Cholesterol and fat control, weight loss
Preventing cellulite formation
Soothing nervous tension, anxiety, insomnia
Acne and skin blemishes
Antibacterial, antifungal, antiseptic
Nausea, menstrual problems
Calming teas and massage oils
Coughs, colds, nasal congestion, pneumonia
Malaria
Aromatherapy

 ## OTHER USES

Perfumes, disinfectants, soaps, hair products.
Pesticides and preservatives.
To repel insects like mosquitoes, fleas and whitefly.

ASAFOETIDA *Ferula foetida*

Growing some two metres (six and a half feet) high and related to carrots, this food of the gods, stinking gum, giant fennel or devil's dung grows in mountains and deserts. Greenish-yellow flowers are followed by flat, oval fruits with a milky juice. The massive roots are thick, pulpy, covered with bristly fibres and, like the stems, yield a strong fetid smell. The resin, which is the source of the spice, is greyish-white when fresh but dries to dark amber. If squeezed, the reddish-yellow flakes give out an oil, used as a condiment and seasoning. Some claim that asafoetida is among the secret ingredients in Worcestershire Sauce. It was one of Alexander the Great's conquering expeditions that brought it back to Europe from Persia but, after the fall of the Roman Empire, it was rare until the 1500s.

SOURCES AND USES			
ORIGINS	**SPREAD**	**TASTE TYPE**	**CULINARY USES**
Eastern Iran and Afghanistan	India	A fetid, sulfurous smell (hence the name) Strong, pungent, bitter, acrid Once cooked, it tastes smooth (like leeks, onions and garlic)	Curries (especially lentil curries like dal) Pickles, relishes, chutneys, papads, vegetable dishes A condiment and flavour enhancer To harmonize sweet, sour, salty and spicy elements

 MORE FOOD FACTS

It is sold in lump or powdered form.
The gum is usually combined with Arabic gum, flour and turmeric.
Mild dried asafoetida can be salted and eaten with salad.
In Afghanistan the huge cabbage-like heads are eaten raw.

 TRADITIONALLY USED FOR

Flatulence, colic pain, constipation
Enhancing appetite, taste, digestion
Healing wounds
Influenza, whooping cough, asthma, bronchitis, colds
Preventing epileptic seizures
A possible opium antidote

 DID YOU KNOW?

The resin is tough to grate – it is traditionally crushed between stones or hit with a hammer.
Wearing a bag of stinking asafoetida around the neck has been inflicted as a punishment but was also said to ward off colds, toothache, Spanish flu and smallpox.
It is one of the pungent vegetables avoided by Buddhist vegetarians.
In Moghul India court singers ate it with butter to improve their voices.

 OTHER USES

It may be used to bait catfish, pike, moths – and wolves.
In Jamaica, asafoetida may be applied to the soft part of a baby's head (the fontanelle) to prevent spirits entering.
It is used in magic spells, to both protect and curse, and to deter demonic forces.

BAY LEAF OR LAUREL *Laurus nobilis*

Bay is officially a herb but the leaves are often treated as a spice and are included in spice lists – they pair well with other spices to enhance their flavours. Once this aromatic, evergreen tree covered much of the Mediterranean area; its green, glossy leaves were an emblem of prosperity in Biblical days and symbolized Christ's resurrection. In ancient Greece a wreath of bay laurels was the prize at the games held in Apollo's honour, and poets and scholars wore bay wreaths when they received academic honours. A laurel wreath also became the Roman victory symbol that was awarded to victorious warriors. The terms *poet laureate* and *baccalaureate* derive from laurel and its association with great achievements.

SOURCES AND USES			
ORIGINS	**SPREAD**	**TASTE TYPE**	**CULINARY USES**
Mediterranean forests	Turkey, Syria, Spain, Portugal, north Europe, Morocco, Canary Islands, Madeira India, China, Indonesia, California	Aromatic, pungent, sharp, bitter	Stocks, soups, stews, braises Pasta, pâté, bouquet garni Seafood, vegetable dishes, sauces Bloody Mary cocktails

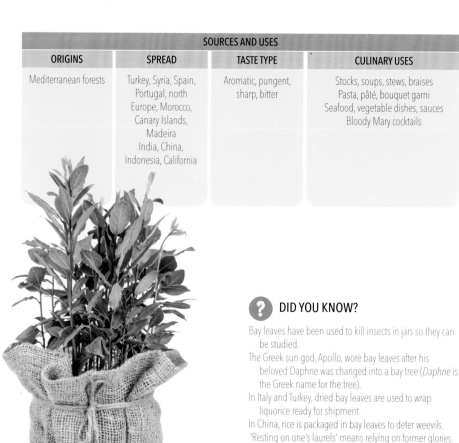

❓ DID YOU KNOW?

Bay leaves have been used to kill insects in jars so they can be studied.

The Greek sun god, Apollo, wore bay leaves after his beloved Daphne was changed into a bay tree (*Daphne* is the Greek name for the tree).

In Italy and Turkey, dried bay leaves are used to wrap liquorice ready for shipment.

In China, rice is packaged in bay leaves to deter weevils. 'Resting on one's laurels' means relying on former glories.

Bay leaves can be scattered among food stores to deter flies, roaches and mice.

The California bay tree (*Umbellularia californica*) is similar to bay but has a stronger taste.

 MORE FOOD FACTS

Compliments chicken, pork, beef and seafood.
Bay wood burnt on barbecues produces a rich scent.

 OTHER USES

Bay rum cologne.
The cleansing oil is antibiotic, antifungal and anti-itching.

 TRADITIONALLY USED FOR

Stomachache, indigestion
Migraines, earache, high blood pressure
Flu, bronchitis
Arthritis, rheumatism
Bruises, wounds
Stinging nettle, poison ivy and poison oak rashes
Bee and wasp stings
Breast and skin cancer

 WARNING

The leaves should be removed before eating as whole leaves can damage the digestive tract
Ground bay leaves *can* be ingested safely

PEPPERMINT *Mentha piperita*

The flowering tops of peppermint are used as well as the leaves so peppermint counts as both spice and herb. This hybrid of watermint and spearmint spreads voraciously underground, sending up vigorous shoots with serrated leaves and whorls of tiny white and purple flowers beloved by honeybees. Mint symbolizes hospitality and friendship. The ancient Greeks and Romans crowned themselves with peppermint at their feasts; it was used to clean banqueting tables and dropped into bathwater as a stimulant. Its name derives from river nymph, Minthe, who caught the eye of Hades, God of the Underworld. His jealous wife turned her into a plant so that everyone would tread over and crush her. Hades granted Minthe a fine aroma so that at least he could still sense her presence! Less romantically, peppermint oil is used in plumbing to test if pipes are fitted tightly and to disclose leaks by its scent.

SOURCES AND USES			
ORIGINS	**SPREAD**	**TASTE TYPE**	**CULINARY USES**
Europe, Middle East, Mediterranean basin	Widespread, in many regions of the world. The USA produces over 70 per cent of global supply	Aromatic and menthol	Adds taste and decoration. Sauces, potatoes, meat (especially lamb). Cocktails, candies, ice cream. Cordials, fruit compotes

 MORE FOOD FACTS

Mint tea is popular in Morocco and North Africa.

 DID YOU KNOW?

Research indicates that sniffing mint improves concentration and memory; several Japanese companies now pipe small amounts through their air conditioning systems to enthuse workers and improve productivity.
Mint has been found in Egyptian tombs dating from 1000 BCE.
Early Romans believed eating mint would increase intelligence.
Mint aromas were said to stop temper tantrums.
Mint was strewn to disguise the rank smell of medieval halls.

 TRADITIONALLY USED FOR

Stomachache, indigestion, heartburn, constipation
Headaches, neuralgia, chest pains
Common colds, respiratory difficulties, catarrh
Bad breath
Minor burns, skin irritations
Irritable bowel syndrome
Antibacterial, anti-inflammatory, cooling

OTHER USES

Toothpaste, shower gel, breath fresheners, perfumes.
After-dinner mints do aid digestion.

ROSE PETALS AND HIPS *Rosa*

Throughout history (and long before!) rose petals – thought to possess magical healing powers and to be an aphrodisiac – have scented both the air and perfumes. Ever a symbol of romance, passion and peace, the rose has been revered, painted, and cultivated in gardens since about 500 BCE in China. Egyptian Queen Cleopatra ordered her bed to be daily strewn with fresh roses and in 42 BCE, to honour Mark Antony's visit, had the floors covered 60 centimetres (two feet) deep in rose petals. Roman Emperor Nero showered his guests with fresh petals – to the point where they almost suffocated. French Emperor Napoleon Bonaparte's military officers were given bags of dry rose petals, for boiling in white wine and applying to gunshot wounds to prevent lead poisoning. The berry-like hips (usually red, purple or black) contain between five and 160 'seeds'; many are relished by fruit-eating birds and are incredibly rich in vitamin C, containing more than any vegetable or fruit.

SOURCES AND USES			
ORIGINS	SPREAD	TASTE TYPE	CULINARY USES
China (a few in Europe, North America, northwest Africa)	All parts of the northern hemisphere; every climate except fully tropical *R. stella* thrives in the desert; *R. acicularis* blooms in the Arctic	Sweet, strawberry-like – or spicy and tart	Jam, jellies, marmalades, rose-hip syrup Cooling rosewater, herbal teas Petals garnish drinks, cocktails, salads, soups, cakes, scones, desserts, ice-cream (including India's *kulfi* ice-cream) Nougat, baklava, gumdrops, Turkish delight, marshmallows, candied rose petals Rose creams (chocolate-covered rose fondant)

 OTHER USES

Perfumes, face packs, skin care, makeup.
Decoration, religious practices.
Scenting bathwater.

 WARNING

Pregnant women should seek medical advice before taking rose hip syrup as it contains vitamin A.

 DID YOU KNOW?

The rose is England's national flower, the USA's floral emblem, and the official flower of New York, Iowa, North Dakota and Georgia.

Even in the 1800s, dried rose petals were still believed to possess mystical powers.

The thousand-year-old rose scrambling up Hildesheim Cathedral, Germany, may be the world's oldest.

The number of petals ranges from four to 200.

Early Christians saw the five *Rosa sancta* petals as symbols of Christ's five wounds.

It takes 2,000 flowers to produce one gram of oil.

R. spinosissima grows in seaside sand; *R. clinophylla* survives six months below the Brahmaputra flood waters in Asia.

Today there are more than 1,000 rose varieties.

Dried petals may retain their perfume for 25 years.

 TRADITIONALLY USED FOR

Heart problems, blood pressure, arthritis
Freshening breath and body odours
Suppressing cancer growth
High cholesterol
Stomach problems (especially *R. chinensis*)
Reducing thirst, lessening gastric inflammation
Diarrhoea, constipation, gallbladder problems and gallstones
Diabetes, urinary tract and kidney disorders
Rose hip syrup wards off colds and flu
Some hips have significant vitamin levels

 MORE FOOD FACTS

The petals of mascena and apothecary roses are used to flavour Indian, Chinese and Middle Eastern dishes.

CLOVES *Syzygium aromaticum* or *Eugenia aromatica*

Cloves are the dried flower buds of an evergreen tree. The pale flower buds turn green, rosy peach, yellow and finally bright red – by which time they are ripe for picking. The flowers have a fresh, strong scent but the entire tree is highly aromatic with the stalks even more pungent than the cloves. We know they have been traded since at least 1721 BCE as a Syrian pot containing cloves dates from then. The spice arrived in Europe between 300 and 500 CE. Muslim sailors and medieval merchants augmented the clove trade and the fictitious Sinbad the Sailor (of *Arabian Nights'* fame) was said to have bought and sold Indian cloves. By the 1600s, the Dutch East India Company controlled much of the spice trade and tried to assert a monopoly over cloves but as the trees grew all over the Moluccas or Spice Islands, this proved impossible.

SOURCES AND USES			
ORIGINS	SPREAD	TASTE TYPE	CULINARY USES
Moluccas (Indonesia)	India, Pakistan, Sri Lanka, Southern Philippines, Madagascar, Tanzania, Zanzibar East and West Indies, Mauritius, Brazil Moluccas and Pemba offer the finest	Aromatic, pungent	Cuisine from Near and Middle East, Asia, Africa Meats, curries, fruit crumbles Marinades Combines well with red wine Compliments apples, pears, rhubarb Hot drinks, especially with lemon and sugar Pairs well with allspice, basil, cinnamon, citrus peel, star anise, peppercorns, vanilla

 MORE FOOD FACTS

Mexican meals often combine cloves with cinnamon and cumin.

 DID YOU KNOW?

In the 1600s, when putrid air was thought to spread bubonic plague, doctors wore beak-like masks filled with cloves, mint and rose petals.
During the third century BCE, a Chinese Han Dynasty ruler ordered all those approaching him to freshen their breath by munching cloves.
Aged between 350 to 400 years, the world's oldest clove tree is on Ternate (Spice Islands).
Each berry has only one seed.

 TRADITIONALLY USED FOR

Indian Ayurvedic, Chinese and herbal medicine
Dentistry and toothache (the essential oil is a painkiller)
Indigestion, hiccough, bronchial problems
Impotence and premature ejaculation
Morning sickness, vomiting, diarrhoea
Multiple sclerosis
Fevers

 OTHER USES

Toothpastes
Indonesian cigarettes and cigars
To make scented pomanders
A mosquito and ant repellent
Anesthetizing fish
It is a strong germicide, antiseptic and astringent
The oil must be kept cool in dark bottles, and is used for toothache

CLAVO
PIMIENTA CINCO BAYAS
PIMIENTA ROSA GRANO
PIMIENTA VERDE GRANO
PIMIENTA NEGRA GRANO
PIMIENTA BLANCA GRANO

100 cc 2€

RAS EL HANOUT
ESPECIAS TÍPICAS GRANADA
CURRY
CURCUMA
AZAFRAN MOLIDO

MIXED SPICES

JENGIBRE RAIZ
MOSTAZA GRANO
AJONJOLIN O SESAMO
ANIS GRANO
VAINILLA MOLI

Indian pickles.

Pickling spice

Pickling began 4,000 years ago in India and is a means of conserving food in brine or vinegar, but the process also adds interesting flavours and so is enjoyed in its own right, not simply because it preserves food for the winter months or for a journey. Pickling may also improve the nutritional value through its introduction of B vitamins. It can be used to preserve vegetables like onions, olives and cucumber or fish like herring. The pickling spice is a mixture of whole and broken spices, seeds, and herbs and most typically includes allspice, bay leaves, black pepper, cinnamon, coriander, dill, bay, fenugreek, ginger, mustard seed, and paprika.

Worcestershire powder and sauce

Worcestershire powder is a dry version of the liquid Worcestershire sauce. Its bitter, slightly sour taste comes from tamarind and can spice up casseroles, soups, grilled meats, chillies, dips and cheese dishes. It also adds pep to Bloody Mary drinks. It is based on an old East Indian recipe brought to the UK in the 1830s. Two dispensing chemists from Worcester, John Wheeley Lea and William Henry Perrins were asked to copy the recipe but when the resulting sauce proved incredibly hot and seemingly inedible, the mixture was left, forgotten in its barrel in a basement, for several years – where it eventually mellowed to a delicious savoury taste. Lea and Perrins Worcester sauce was born – rediscovered and marketed highly successfully. Today it is still aged in wooden casks for 18 months.

Ingredients: tamarind soaked in molasses, vinegar, spice, salt, sugar, tomato, garlic, anchovies, caramel, sumac, cloves, shallots, pepper, hickory smoke, lemons, pickles, peppers and cayenne.

Lea and Perris' UK sauce uses malt vinegar while the US version uses distilled white vinegar. The mixture is best left to mellow over two years, given just the occasional stir – then sieved and either bottled to make sauce or dried to make powder.

Mixed (pudding) spice

This mix of sweet spices is used in baking, desserts and for fruit, particularly in Britain and her former colonies. The mix generally contains cinnamon, allspice and nutmeg. Possible additional spices include coriander, cloves, ginger, honey, ground mace, coriander and ginger.

Mulling spices

This European spice mixture of cinnamon, cloves, allspice, nutmeg and dried fruit is used to infuse wine or punch with warming spices, often given to Christmas guests and carollers.

American pumpkin (or apple pie) spice

Pumpkin pie is a traditional sweet dessert often eaten in the USA at Thanksgiving and at Christmas in both the USA and Canada. Pumpkins were exported to France and introduced to Tudor England,

Mulled wine.

but apple pie has long been a traditional dessert, and enjoys the same spice treatment, a blend of cinnamon, clove, nutmeg, and allspice.

Chilli powder

This is not simply powdered chilli, but a blend of powdered red chilli peppers and other spices and herbs, such as cumin, coriander, oregano, paprika, cloves or allspice, red cayenne pepper and garlic. It is often used in Mexican and Tex-Mex cooking. Between three and eight dried chillies will be needed and can be in whatever combination suits to include: *Ancho*, *pasilla* or *mulato* (mild); *New Mexico*/*ristra* or *cascabel* (medium); *Chiltepin* (very hot).

Curry powder

Curry powder is a Western imposition; there is nothing actually called curry powder in South Asia but the basic mix with which we are now familiar comprises turmeric, chilli powder, ground coriander, ground cumin, ground ginger and pepper. A 'sweet' curry powder will include these basics plus cinnamon, cloves and paprika.

Chilli and paprika.

A TO Z OF OTHER MIXED SPICES

Advieh: used in Persian and Mesopotamian cuisines – turmeric, cinnamon, cardamom, cloves, rose petals or rose buds, cumin, and ginger … plus possibly saffron, nutmeg, black pepper, mace, sesame or coriander.

Cajun spices: cumin, coriander and paprika plus, possibly, oregano, salt and/or cracked pepper.

Chinese five-spice powder: a blend of cassia (Chinese cinnamon), star anise and cloves, plus fennel and Sichuan peppercorns. Some recipes also contain ginger and nutmeg, while cardamom, cayenne, cloves and fenugreek might also be added.

Garam masala: an Indian savoury spice blend of cumin, coriander, cardamom, pepper, cinnamon, cloves and nutmeg, used particularly in north India and Pakistan.

Goda masala: a sweet spice blend used in the southwestern part of the Indian peninsula, usually including cardamom, cinnamon, cloves, bay leaf, white sesame seeds, coriander seeds, coconut flakes, cassia buds, dagad phool (lichen) and white and black peppercorns.

Hawaij: Yemenite ground spice mixtures primarily for soups and coffee. For soup, use pepper, cumin, cardamom, caraway, turmeric, cloves, coriander seeds and leaves. For coffee, desserts and cakes, use aniseed, fennel seeds, ginger and cardamom

Jerk seasoning: The usual base for this dry meat rub or marinade mix is allspice (pimento) and Scotch bonnet peppers. The seasoning sometimes also includes brown sugar, cloves, cinnamon, garlic, ginger, nutmeg, salt, scallions and thyme. Now a Jamaican specialty, it may be of pre-slavery African origins – and is very hot. As well as meat like beef, chicken, sausage and lamb, it can be used with fish, shrimps, shellfish and vegetables.

Kaala masala: black spice blend from the Indian subcontinent using dark roasted spices – cumin, sesame and coriander seeds, clove, cinnamon sticks, coconut and chillies.

Kanda lasun masala: a hot spice blend, mainly used in the southwestern Indian peninsula, with sun-dried red chillies, garlic, onion, coconut and other spices.

Khmeli suneli: a blend used in Georgia and the Caucasus region mixing marjoram, dill, summer savory, mint, parsley, coriander, fenugreek leaves, ground marigold petals, black pepper, ground fenugreek seeds, and crushed bay leaves.

Lemon pepper: lemon zest and black pepper are baked, crushed and seasoned with salt.

Mitmita: an orange-red, powdered seasoning mix used in Ethiopian and Eritrean cuisine containing ground African birdseye chilli peppers, cardamom seed, cloves and salt.

Montreal steak seasoning: a dry rub mix for steaks and grilled meats, typically including garlic, coriander, black pepper, dill seed, salt and Cayenne pepper flakes.

Panch phoron: a Bengali five-spice blend of whole fenugreek, nigella, fennel, cumin, and mustard or radhuni seeds.

Poultry seasoning: an American blend of predominantly sage, with savory, thyme, marjoram, rosemary – and perhaps celery seed, onion powder, nutmeg or any other seasonings used when cooking chicken or turkey.

Quatre épices: French blend of ground pepper, cloves, nutmeg and ginger.

Ras el hanout: North African blend that includes cinnamon and cumin among other spices.

Salt: seasoned salt can be livened up with black pepper, ground paprika, minced or powdered onion, celery seed, parsley and various dried spices such as mustard, oregano and garlic. Other additions could include thyme, turmeric, cumin powder, marjoram, red cayenne pepper, crushed or ground rosemary and ground white pepper.

Shichimi: Japanese blend of seven spices: red chilli pepper, sansho or Sichuan pepper, dried citrus peel, sesame seeds (white and black) hemp seeds and ginger... plus nori or aonori. Garlic and poppy seeds might also be added.

Taco seasoning: chilli powder, garlic powder, onion powder, ginger, crushed red pepper flakes, dried oregano, paprika, ground cumin, sea salt and black pepper perhaps with a touch of cumin, coriander, cardamom, cinnamon, cloves and nutmeg.

Tandoori masala: South Asian spice blend for tandoori cooked meats. Blend the spices with yogurt and lime juice for a delicious marinade using coriander, salt, fenugreek, onion powder, black pepper, chilli, garlic powder, cassia, cinnamon, cumin, ginger, clove, bay leaves, nutmeg, celery powder and cardamom.

Vadouvan: perhaps inspired by France's colonial period in Puducherry, India, this

French 'masala' blend includes chopped onions and shallots, garlic cloves, vegetable oil, fenugreek seeds, ground cumin, ground cardamom, brown mustard seeds, turmeric, grated nutmeg, hot red-pepper flakes and ground cloves.

Za'atar: this is both an individual herb with a thyme-like flavour from Syrian-Lebanese mountains and a spice blend of the herb mixed with sesame seeds, chopped fresh oregano, dried marjoram, ground sumac, sea salt and ground cumin.

Garam masala.

THE STORY OF SALT

Salt is not, by definition, a spice but has graced our tables, alongside mustard and pepper, for centuries and played a vital part in human lives. It adds flavour, spikes the taste buds and – until the dawn of domestic refrigeration in the early 1900s – was the main means of preserving food. Previously, at the onset of winter, when fresh food for livestock became scarce, many animals were slaughtered and their meat had to be kept throughout the season. It was not until the seventeenth-century Agrarian Revolution that crop rotation and winter feeds (like turnips and clover) were thoroughly understood and implemented, allowing cattle to be overwintered. So salting foods ensured supplies lasted through the coldest months and could also be transported over long distances.

Salt has been a major contributor to human survival and culture; it has been the subject of many fairy tales and is often attributed magical powers. The quest for salt has invoked bitter warfare as well as the establishment of long-distance trade routes.

Water and rock

Salt is not easily obtained. The two main sources are seawater and rock salt. It can be extracted from the ocean or dried-up seas; sometimes it bubbles to the surface as brine (to be transformed into salt crystals by evaporation) or forms salt licks or shallow caverns. It can be evaporated from salt pans, boiled down from brine, or mined from white salt veins, sometimes hundreds of metres deep beneath the Earth's surface. It was not until the later nineteenth century that industrial mining and new drilling techniques were able to expose deeper deposits. When Julius Caesar invaded Britain in 55 BCE, he found the locals pouring brine over hot sticks and then scraping off the leftover glaze, an inefficient method compared to that used by Caesar's salinators who were skilled at boiling brine to provide salt for his troops.

Salt collecting in a time-honoured, traditional manner.

China's innovations

The northern province of Shanxi is the site of China's earliest salt works and saw countless wars over its control. Historians have found that as early as 6000 BCE (possibly even sooner), salt was harvested from the surface of Lake Yuncheng in that province after the summer evaporation.

Even some 4,700 years ago, the different kinds of salts and methods of extraction were understood by the Chinese; one treatise listed more than 40 kinds. One early system was to fill clay containers with water from the ocean and boil them until only the sought-after salt remained. But by 450 BCE boiling brine in iron pans had become the main process. It spread through Europe via the Roman Empire about 1,000 years later, and remained the main system in China for nearly 2,000 years, being still in operation in the nineteenth century.

China spearheaded salt economics – both tax and trade. Salt drove technological development and proved a stable source of revenue for the imperial government. It was China's major cash crop: whoever controlled salt controlled almost everything else.

Other nations, towns and names

Vast underground salt beds occur in many parts of the USA, Canada and the UK. Salt deposits have often inspired place names: Salzburg in Austria had vital salt mines and its name means the 'City of Salt'; Tuzla (in Bosnia and Herzegovina) means 'place of salt'.

England's Liverpool rose from a small town to a major port as the salt that was dug in nearby Cheshire salt mines became vital to nineteenth-century trade. Several English places carry the suffix 'wich' (that mutated from meaning a trading place, excavation, brine springs or wells to eventually imply salt production) including Middlewich, Nantwich and Droitwich.

Possibly the earliest known town in Europe, Solnitsata, (in today's Bulgaria) rose around its salt production and supply line to the Balkans, where salt making was very important. Meanwhile, salt mines in Poland led to a vast sixteenth-century kingdom – undermined only when the Germans brought in sea salt. Then cities like Munich flourished. Venice rose to its economic prime through its salt monopoly; the city fought Genoa over salt but ironically the Italians Christopher Columbus and John Cabot (sailing for Spain and England respectively) would later destroy the Mediterranean trade by bringing the New World's resources into the marketplace.

Routes and roads

At first it was animals that trod down paths leading to salt licks but as people followed so these well-worn trails became salt roads, in regular use by the Bronze Age. Soon settlements and towns sprang up beside them.

Readily available salt was rare and precious, its importance swelling side by side with civilization. As Rome expanded, so roads were built to enable more efficient transportation of trade goods to the city. One of the busiest was the Via Salaria, the salt route from the Adriatic, over which soldiers marched while merchants drove oxcarts full of the 'white gold'.

During the late Roman Empire and medieval times, salt was transported in vast caravans, some routes uniting the salt oases of the Libyan desert. Thousands of camels every year trudged across the Sahara bearing salt inland or trading it for slaves: Timbuktu was a huge salt and slave market; merchants there in the twelfth century valued salt as highly as books and gold.

Salt routes crisscrossed the globe, including the seas; ships bearing salt from Egypt to Greece sailed across the Mediterranean and the Aegean. In the sixth century, Moorish merchants traded salt for gold in sub-Saharan Africa – ounce for ounce, or even more. Later, the Venetians exchanged salt in Constantinople for Asian spices.

Halle in Germany is set on an old salt route, connecting German salt mines to Baltic shipping ports. France produced salt, too, and has its own salt road along the Mediterranean coast. Cities, states and duchies exacted hefty duties and taxes for the salt passing through their territories as the ebb and flow of salt and its monetary implications spurred population movements, invasions and wars.

Salt as currency

Once upon a time this highly valued commodity served as currency. Roman soldiers were paid in salt, hence the saying 'worth his salt' and the word 'salary' – from *salarium* (salt-money: payment to soldiers for – or in – salt). Rock-salt slabs in Abyssinia and cakes of salt in central Africa also served as coinage.

In 1295 the Italian traveller Marco Polo delighted the Venetian Doge with tales of the prodigious value of salt in China and how salt cake coins were stamped with the great Kublai Khan's imperial seal. In the American–British War of 1812, the money-strapped American government paid their soldiers with salt brine. Nomads in Ethiopia's Danakil Plains still use salt as money.

Traditions and sayings

The Old Testament describes how salt was added to burnt animal sacrifices and that accepting salt from someone meant being in that person's service, while in the New Testament Jesus said, 'You are the salt of the earth', reflecting the value of his disciples and how they would be called upon to preserve the world from moral decay.

Other familiar phrases include to, 'rub salt in a wound … salt an invoice … take it with a grain of salt'. Offering bread and salt to visitors is still a traditional sign of hospitality in many places.

❓ DID YOU KNOW?

Native Americans in the Caribbean harvested sea salt.

In ancient Mexico, women wearing garlands of wormwood in their hair performed a ritual dance in honour of the Goddess of Salt.

Every cell in the body contains salt, which also carries signals to and from (and within) the brain.

Overdosing with salt was used as a method of ritual suicide in China.

This valuable commodity attracted profiteers and the black market saw smuggling rings, riots and revolutions. In 1785, Britain's earl of Dundonald wrote that each year 10,000 people were seized for salt smuggling and 300 men were sent to the gallows for contraband trade in salt and tobacco.

Aware of the preserving qualities of salt, Taoist monk-alchemists in the 800s, seeking immortality, discovered saltpetre which soon became an essential element of gunpowder, leading to the Chinese making the world's first firearms.

In ancient Greece, the 'Father of Medicine', Hippocrates (c.460–370 BCE) advocated immersing patients in sea salt water to heal various ailments.

In Roman religious rituals, grains of salt were rubbed on an eight-day-old baby's lips to keep away demons and evil spirits.

Salt is an effective antiseptic, hence the Roman word (sal) is related to Salus, the goddess of health.

Roman vestal virgins prepared temple sacrificial millstones by rubbing them with brine.

It wasn't just the Armada! The Dutch blockade of Iberian saltworks led to Spanish bankruptcy and King Philip II's slide from power and wealth.

Ancient military conquerors, including Assyrians and Hebrews, ritually spread salt on places they had subdued to curse the inhabitants.

The word 'salad' comes from salt: the ancient Romans salted leafy greens and vegetables.

In the American Revolutionary War, Americans who supported Britain intercepted salt shipments to disable the preservation of revolutionaries' food.

During India's independence movement, Mahatma Gandhi defied British salt laws and so mobilized popular support for India's self-rule.

In the Bible, when Lot's wife had a moment of doubt and turned to look back at Sodom, she was transformed into a pillar of salt.

Egyptian art from 1450 BCE depicts salt making and preserving meat and fish with salt. The divine salt, natron, was used to preserve Egyptian mummies; ordinary salt was used to mummify lesser mortals and for offerings such as jars of salt or salted vegetables and fruits.

For five centuries the French had to buy all their salt from royal depots and so pay the salt tax, (*gabelle*), a major grievance that contributed to the French Revolution.

Spilling salt is regarded as an ill omen: in Leonardo da Vinci's painting *The Last Supper*, Judas is shown with an upturned saltcellar in front of him.

In medieval etiquette, which endured right up until the 1700s, important guests at banquets sat at the head of the table 'above the salt'. People who sat 'below the salt', farthest from the host, were the 'also rans'!

The Erie Canal (completed in 1825 to connect the Great Lakes of North America to New York's Hudson River) was called 'the ditch that salt built'. Salt tax revenues paid for half the cost of its construction.

Thousands of troops died during French Emperor Napoleon Bonaparte's retreat from Moscow in 1812 because of salt shortages: they had lowered resistance to disease and their wounds did not heal.

Throwing salt over your shoulder after a funeral scares off any evil spirits that may be clinging to your back. A handful of salt may be thrown into the coffin *before* the burial to repel the devil.

A gift of salt is a symbol of good luck in India.

Before sumo wrestlers begin their matches, a handful of salt is thrown into the ring to drive off malevolent spirits.

Hopi legends claim that salt deposits are set far from civilization to make tapping its riches a punishing challenge.

In 1933, the Dalai Lama was buried sitting up in a bed of salt.

Salt was added in beer brewing in ancient Scotland to stop it being ruined by witches and evil spirits. The salt *did* prevent excessive fermentation and corruption.

Elephants dig up earth, hollow out deep caverns, and carve out hillsides to reach salt licks and minerals.

THE SPICE TRADE

*'You can never cross the ocean unless you have
the courage to lose sight of the shore.'*
Christopher Columbus (1451–1506) Genoa, Italy

Once upon a time, exotic spices were, indeed, the stuff of fairy tales – worth a good deal more than the food they enhanced. Nutmegs, for example, were more valuable than their weight in gold. Therein lay the motive that inspired voyages into unknown waters, the courage to face fierce seas, unexpected dangers, rivalry and battles. The adventurous spirit was stirred by the chance to accrue great riches and so many an intrepid explorer and ambitious merchant set out in search of new spices – and new routes to discover these treasures. The Spice Trade was one of the most important in the world, responsible for raising and destroying empires. Ultimately, it led to the discovery of unknown continents and entirely different cultures as well as a completely new vision and understanding of our globe.

Back as early as 3,000 BCE, India's southwest, especially Kerala, was laying the foundation of the ancient spice trade routes from the East Indies. This was followed by Greco-Roman trading along the Incense Route, a network of both land and sea trading links between the Mediterranean world and the lure of incense and spices like cinnamon, cassia, ginger, nutmeg, cloves, mace and pepper that lay further east and south. The Roman Empire oversaw all the spices entering the Greco-Roman world from a powerful trading centre in Alexandria, Egypt, set up in the first century BCE. There was much secrecy: traders did not disclose their sources and wove great mystery and fantastic tales around both the spices themselves and the magical places where they grew. There were even stories of fierce winged creatures that guarded spices growing high on cliff walls.

Indians and Ethiopians dominated the Red Sea routes but by the mid-seventh century CE the rise of Islam closed off the overland caravan routes through Egypt and the Suez, preventing European access. Arab traders took over, conveying goods to Europe via the southwest Asian Levant and the ever-more dominant Venice merchants. Baghdad became a centre for trade and Arabia took on its own allure with tales like *Sinbad the Sailor* and *Aladdin*.

The route the spices took from the East Indies was protracted and dangerous; typhoons, sandstorms and pirates added to the hazards. The spices were generally harvested by slaves, and then sailed or paddled in tiny vessels from the Spice Islands of Indonesia (the Moluccas) to Malacca in Malaysia. Next they were shipped in junks across several treacherous tropical seas – then carried on camelback through the hot, arid desert from Aden to Egypt, becoming more expensive with each additional hard-won mile. Emirs and sultans took their share in customs tariffs on the exotic freight while pirates were likely to seize the spices as booty or demand a ransom before the spices at last arrived into the hands of European merchants in Alexandria or Constantinople.

From the eighth century until the fifteenth, Venice, Genoa and other European maritime republics jealously guarded the monopoly of Europe's trade with the Middle East. Desirable but expensive commodities – including spices, silk, herbs, incense, drugs, medicines and opium – were all imported from Asia and Africa and made the Mediterranean city-states incredibly rich and powerful.

All this was to change when in 1453 the Ottoman Turks seized Constantinople and slammed the gates shut, barring Europeans from vital land-sea routes. Now the powerful Muslim traders dominated maritime spice trading routes throughout the Indian Ocean.

Suddenly there was even stronger motivation to discover new routes and more direct sources, ultimately inspiring the Age of Discovery. Portugal's Prince Henry the Navigator sent ships to explore Africa's western coast in the early and mid-fifteenth century, and the Portuguese explorer and navigator Vasco da Gama first set sail from Europe around the Cape of Good Hope to reach the Indian Ocean in 1498, thus opening up new maritime routes to reach the alluring stores of pepper and other precious spices. The Indies' wealth was now open for the Europeans to explore, with Portugal the first European seaborne empire to emerge from the spice trade. Now many nations struggled to gain control of the trade along the mutating spice routes while the Dutch simply bypassed all these profiteers by taking a direct ocean route from the Cape to Indonesia.

In due course, Christopher Columbus set out to sail in totally the opposite direction to try and reach the East Indies that way and discover a fresh route to the spices, claiming 'But in truth, should I meet with gold or spices in great quantity, I shall remain till I collect as much as possible, and for this purpose I am proceeding solely in quest of them.' In so doing, he discovered the Americas, landing in the Bahamas in 1492.

Suddenly here was a New World, with hitherto unknown plants to add to the riches of both European cuisine and the swelling coffers of the merchants and traders. Now there was another magnet for pirates and profiteers, a source of silver and gold, tobacco, sugar, cocoa, tomatoes, allspice, wild ginger and vanilla.

Many more voyagers and explorers followed Columbus including Vasco Núñez de Balboa, Pedro Álvares Cabral (who was aiming for India but was blown westwards towards Brazil) and Ferdinand Magellan who reached the Pacific and ultimately the Spice Islands, too, and whose fleet was the first to circumnavigate the globe. Now there was an altogether opposite route to reach the spices, a global circuit linking Asia, the Americas and Europe. A vast trade network would soon stretch from Manila in the Philippines, via Mexico and Central America, to Spain and the rest of Europe.

In the battles for control in this new geography, and especially the lucrative trade in nutmeg (indigenous to the volcanic soils of the Indonesian Banda Islands), the Portuguese annexed these islands in 1512 but in due course were themselves ousted by the Dutch who hoped to secure a secure a monopoly when in 1602 they drew up a treaty with village chiefs. However, the Bandanese nutmeg growers continued selling to other traders.

By the eighteenth century the USA had begun its entry into the world spice industry, establishing their own spice companies and dealing directly with Asian growers; soon hundreds of American ships were sailing around the world to collect spices. Meanwhile, Texas settlers created chilli powder as an easier way to make spicy Mexican dishes. Eventually, with improved transport, open trade routes, greater availability and better transplanting skills, spice values dropped. Even the wealthiest monopolies were undermined by the increased flow of the once so-elusive spices.

Today pepper and cinnamon are stocked in every kitchen. The allure and secrecy that had made them the world's most valuable items, alongside gold and jewels, is no longer a potent force. None the less, the wonderful flavours, colours and aromas still remain as vibrant as ever, adding an exotic edge to our cuisine.

Spreading the flavours

Because of India's strategic position in relation to the spice routes and controls, many Indian merchants were involved in the trade and introduced their cuisine to Southeast Asia, especially Malaysia and Indonesia, where curries and spice mixtures were absorbed into the culture.

Moreover many Europeans involved in the spice trade or travelling to these exotic parts of the world made friends or intermarried with Indians, and so learned about and spread valuable local culinary know-how and ingredients – with recipes suitably adapted to the European palate. Some rather exclusive establishments had appeared in England by 1811, catering to the tastes of those returning from India and to other gourmets curious to explore such a different cuisine. This was a two-way exchange, of course and, for example, the Portuguese introduced vinegar to India (Franciscan priests made it from coconut toddy). Traditional British dishes such as roast beef were adapted by the addition of Indian spices like red chilllies and cumin. Other meats and fish were cooked as a curry with local vegetables. Anglo-Indian food often involved yogurt, almonds, coconut and other such regional ingredients. Breads and rice were spiced with distinctive flavours, bringing out the best of the cultural medley and local specialities.

It was World War II that brought even more international foods to America as US soldiers discovered new tastes while they were posted to Europe and Asia. The 'pizza herb', oregano, grew in popularity some 5,200 per cent in the 1940s and early '50s in America. The taste buds were in exploration mode!

Asia is still the source of many of the most famous spices such as cinnamon, pepper, nutmeg, cloves, and ginger. However, many more spices, herbs and aromatic seeds are now cultivated in the West. California grows many herbs; Canada produces aromatic seeds; Nicaragua, El Salvador and the United States have crops of sesame seed; Brazil is a major supplier of pepper. Grenada cultivates nutmeg and Jamaica is a vital source of ginger and allspice. Spices flourish in Europe, too, but the United States is now the world's major spice buyer, followed by Germany, Japan, and France.

It is hard to imagine now just how revered these strange, dusty powders once were. Their value to the sellers sometimes tempted them to cheat. Antique spice merchant recipe books explain just how to dilute valuable spices – how to cut pepper with dirt and stones, or ginger with pinewood sawdust. Such undertakings, however, were dangerous and could invoke severe retribution for those caught in the act. Spice merchants who sold substitute saffron were burned at the stake – along with their imposter spices.

Now there are health and safety officers and trade description acts to protect the public but with spices readily available and no longer worth more than their weight in gold, we can safely browse the supermarket shelves and collect an enormous variety of seasonings, with multiple flavours and aromas, to spike our palates and bring the essence of exotic places into our homes.

❓ DID YOU KNOW?

The spice trade began in the Middle East over 4,000 years ago.

When the Visigoths captured Rome in 410 CE, they demanded 3,000 pounds of peppercorns as ransom.

London dockworkers were paid their bonuses in cloves in the sixteenth century.

The wonders of ports like Lisbon and Amsterdam and rich palaces of Venice and Genoa, were established largely through spice-trade profits.

The word 'buccaneer' comes from the South American and Caribbean Arawak peoples' term *boucan* for the allspice that cured their fish and meats; pirates calling in at Jamaica adopted both the food and the new name.

Mercantile bankers like the Fugger and Welser families of southern Germany accumulated enormous wealth through the spice trade, replacing the de Medici family with their political power and influence.

Pepper was once so valuable that it could be used to pay the rent.

In the 1300s, a pound of nutmeg in Europe was a more valuable commodity than gold, costing the same as seven fattened oxen.

Elihu Yale, once employed as a clerk by the British East India Company in India, began his own spice business and the fortune he made enabled him to launch Yale University.

Nutmegs once fuelled a war that led to Great Britain owning Long Island in New York state, USA.

FASCINATING FACTS

MAGIC, WITCHCRAFT AND SUPERSTITION

In Nigeria grains of paradise are used for divination and for ordeals that determine guilt or innocence.

In Persia, wronged wives put cardamom, cloves and cinnamon into a jar and then recited a passage from the Koran backwards – seven times. The husband's shirt (together with a piece of paper bearing his name and those of four angels) was left to steep in a jar filled with rosewater. Finally, the mixture was heated over a fire until it boiled, by which time the husband's affections would be sure to return.

If you are foolish enough to burn salt, when you die you will be forced to pick every grain of it out of Hell.

If you spill salt, you need to toss some over your right shoulder (and then your left) in order to avoid bad luck.

If you want to prevent the evil eye, bad luck, demons, werewolves and vampires, you should always carry some garlic in your pockets.

On St. Luke's Day, in order to dream of a future partner, women took marigold flowers, a sprig of marjoram, thyme, and a little wormwood and dried these by the fire. They then powdered the mixture, sifted it through fine lawn cloth, and simmered it over a slow fire, adding vinegar and honey. Once it cooled, they would anoint themselves with this liquid and settle to

Wormwood.

sleep – but only after saying the following lines three times:
Saint Luke, Saint Luke, be kind to me,
In dreams let me my true-love see.

Wolf's claw or club moss (*Lycopodium clavatum*) was regarded as magical by Celtic druids and called 'Druids flour'. Because it explodes with a bright flash when thrown onto flames, it was used through the following centuries by mystics, magicians and theatre performers to impress onlookers.

During the Middle Ages it was believed that cumin kept chickens and lovers from wandering off. It was also said that couples that carried cumin seed at their weddings would live together happily.

Carrying turmeric root in your pocket, or tying it on a yellow silk thread around your neck, will protect you from disease.

In past centuries wormwood was said to counteract not only hemlock and toadstool poisoning but also the bites of sea dragons!

Mexicans celebrated their Goddess of Salt Festival with a ceremonial dance by women wearing wormwood garlands and crowns.

ANISEED

Nineteenth-century Germans often flavored their bread with whole aniseed (anise).

Anise is put on fishing lures to attract a catch.

Anise is an ingredient in dog food.

Added to cold water, anise liqueur makes a most refreshing summer drink.

Anise attracts dogs, fish and bees but is poisonous to pigeons.

Classical writers Dioscorides, Theophrastus, Pliny and Paladus enthused about anise.

Anise has been cultivated in English gardens from the mid-1500s but the seeds ripen only in very warm summers.

In the American Civil War anise seeds served as an early form of antiseptic but caused high levels of toxicity in the blood.

Cardamom.

CARDAMOM

In India cardamom fruits are washed with water from special wells and then dried on house-roofs.

In Alexandria in 176 CE cardamom was listed among the Indian spices liable for duty.

In perfumes, it combines well with the aroma of cypress.

In Geoffrey Chaucer's *Canterbury Tales*, cardamom is referred to as 'the spice of paradise'.

Aniseed.

Celery.

CELERY

In ancient Greece winning athletes were presented with bunches of celery.

In 1664 English diarist, John Evelyn, spelled this new arrival 'sellery'.

Celery has been lauded as an aphrodisiac since Roman times.

In Roman times celery was dedicated to Pluto, god of the Underworld and ruler of the dead!

Madame de Pompadour, renowned mistress of French King Louis XV, enjoyed celery and truffle soup followed by hot chocolate.

COCONUTS

A 70-year-old coconut tree may have more than 3,600 roots.

In World War II, a message inscribed on a husked coconut shell was sent by the shipwrecked and wounded crew of a torpedo boat commanded by future US president, John F. Kennedy. This coconut was later kept on the president's desk.

The roots are used as both dye and mouthwash.

A frayed root can be used as a toothbrush.

Ground coconut shell can help remove dead skin.

The ash of dried burned coconut leaves is a source of lime.

The fresh husk of a brown coconut serves as a sponge.

Coconut is a source of lauric acid used in shower gels and shampoos.

In the Philippines, halved coconut shells – with cooked sweet rice and half a boiled egg on top – serve as an offering to the deceased and one's ancestors.

Decorated coconuts are used in Hindu rituals and offered during worship to a god or goddess.

Coconut.

Indian fishermen often offer a coconut to the rivers and seas to be certain of bountiful catches.

Hindus may initiate the beginning of a new enterprise by breaking a coconut to ensure the blessings of the gods and success.

Lakshmi, Hindu goddess of wellbeing and wealth, is often shown holding a coconut.

Coconut flowers are auspicious symbols in India and feature at Hindu and Buddhist weddings and other important ceremonies. In Kerala, coconut flowers *must* be present during a marriage ceremony.

In New Orleans Mardi Gras parades, hand-decorated coconuts may be handed out to the crowd.

The coconut is a target and prize in traditional British fairground coconut shy stalls.

Some Asian myths describe how the first ever girl emerged from coconut blossom.

Technically the coconut fruit is a drupe (a fleshy fruit with a central stone), not a nut.

Coconut water is recommended today as a sports drink as it contains good levels of vitamins, minerals, energy-boosting sugars, dietary fibre, proteins and antioxidants.

Coconut water serves as a growth supplement in plant tissue culture.

Coconut milk has a high fat content of around 17 per cent, but is low in sugars. It is frequently added to curries and other savoury dishes.

The coconut seed's white, fleshy part is called coconut meat and contains manganese, potassium and copper.

Coconut meat is used fresh or dried and is especially tasty in confections and desserts such as macaroons.

Halved, drained coconuts can be hung up as bird feeders, and once the flesh has gone, can be filled with fat in winter to attract birds like bluetits.

Coconut is currently used as a fuel in the Philippines.

Coconut oils contain four growth hormones, which help the development of many organisms.

Coconut-fired carbon filters noxious substances and is used in gas masks and to clean up radiation.

Seeking to impress Pope John Paul II during his visit to the Philippines, President Ferdinand Marcos had an opulent palace built of coconut lumber.

Cosmas, a fifth-century Egyptian traveller to India and Sri Lanka, described an 'Indian nut' that may have been a coconut.

In the ninth century an Arab merchant, Soleyman described the Chinese using coir fibre (extracted from the husk of coconuts) and making toddy.

FLAX

The 'fine linen' mentioned in the Bible was spun from flax.

Flax. Facing page: Honeycomb.

According to Germanic legend, the plant was under the care of the goddess Hulda, who first taught mortals the art of spinning and weaving flax.

Ultimately, the rise of cotton cloth and then synthetic fibres diminished the status of flax.

Linseed has been used to adulterate pepper.

GRAINS OF PARADISE

In West Africa, grains of paradise seeds are chewed on cold days to warm the body.

These seeds (said to have grown in the Garden of Eden) supposedly bring good luck to gamblers, who chew on the seeds and then spit them out into their hands before throwing the dice.

HONEY

Foraging bees have to fly some 88,500 kilometres (55,000 miles), visiting perhaps 2 million flowers to produce just 450 grams (one pound) of honey.

The honeybee is the only insect that produces a food regularly enjoyed by human beings.

In Africa the greater honeyguide bird's calls and actions guide Bushmen to wild beehives; the Bushmen always thank the bird with its own share of the honey.

Humans (and animals like bears, gorillas and honey badgers) will risk vicious stings and sometimes tumbling from high trees in order to gather the precious sweet food.

Honey was vital before the advent of sugar in our diets and was an integral sweetening ingredient in many ancient Roman recipes.

Ancient Egyptians used honey as food and medicine, for offerings and for embalming the dead, while beeswax was used for magic rites, preserving and medication.

Honey is the main ingredient in mead or honey wine; honey's naturally occurring yeast promotes fermentation. Honey is also used in some beers.

Humans apparently began hunting for honey at least 8,000 years ago. Mesolithic rock-paintings in caves near Valencia, Spain, show honey-hunters carrying baskets or gourds and climbing ropes and ladders to gather the honey and honeycomb from a wild bees' nest.

Honey is often used as an ointment for rashes and burns, as a non-toxic antiseptic on pet's wounds and to soothe sore throats and colds.

Fossils of honeybees date back about 150 million years!

Mulberry.

MULBERRY

The Roman naturalist and writer Pliny the Elder called mulberry the Wise Fruit because it flowers only after the last winter frost.

The upper surface of red mulberry leaves is, unlike the lustrous leaves of its white counterpart, as rough as sandpaper.

Mulberry leaves can be fed to livestock.

Vincent van Gogh painted *The Mulberry Tree* in 1889 whilst in hospital in Provence.

MUSTARD

The ancient Greek philosopher Pythagoras (570–c.490 BCE) prescribed it for scorpion stings, while his compatriot Hippocrates (460–377 BCE) used it as a medicine and for mustard poultices.

Nicholas Culpepper, the seventeenth-century English herbalist, considered it good for snake and mushroom poison, if taken promptly.

In the fifth century BCE a grieving mother took her son's body to the Buddha who asked her to bring a handful of mustard seeds from a family that had never lost a child, husband, parent, or friend. Unable to find such a family, she realized her grief was selfish.

Mustard was used in 'Merry England' and was described in 1390 in a book written by one of King Richard II's master cooks.

From the 1500s onwards, coarse-ground mustard seed was mixed with cinnamon and flour, then moistened, rolled into balls and dried – these mustard balls were easily stored and, once needed, could be combined with vinegar or wine to make mustard paste.

Brown mustard, which originated in the Himalayas, is the basic Chinese restaurant mustard.

Mustard.

Mustard flowers can be enjoyed as edible decorations.

Benjamin Franklin may have brought mustard from France to the USA in 1758.

Nutmeg.

NUTMEG

It is claimed that unscrupulous traders from Connecticut, USA would whittle false nutmeg from timber, creating a 'wooden nutmeg', a term that later came to mean any type of fraud. Connecticut is still nicknamed the Nutmeg State.

Nutmeg spice can be baked into pumpkin pies, kneaded into sausages and sprinkled into eggnog.

Prior to the 1700s, the much prized nutmeg could be found only in the Moluccas (the Spice Islands) of Indonesia, and, in order to protect this valuable crop, the Dutch East India Company banned the export of the trees, drenched all the nutmegs in lime before shipping to make them infertile, and imposed the death penalty on anyone suspected of stealing nutmegs or growing and selling them independently – ultimately beheading almost every Bandanese male over the age of 15. The local population was decimated to preserve the company's monopoly over the crop.

Nutmeg was also used as an incense and a medicine that was said to cure stomach ailments, headaches or fever and thought to ward off plague.

At one point in the 1300s, a pound of nutmeg cost seven fattened oxen.

The Dutch monopoly did not include one nutmeg-producing island held by the British, called Run, but a swap for Run in the mid-1600s included granting the British the trading post of Manhattan, where New York would develop.

In 1769, a French horticulturist managed to smuggle some precious nutmeg from the Banda islands to Mauritius, finally ending the Dutch stranglehold.

In due course, the British East India Company brought nutmeg trees to Penang, Singapore, India, the West Indies – and Grenada (now its second largest producer).

PAPRIKA

The word paprika, first used in England in 1896, comes from Serbian, Croatian and

Paprika peppers.

Hungarian origins.
Paprika was brought to Hungary during the Turkish occupation.
Due to the favourable climate and geographical conditions, Hungarian paprika has a bright red colour and a distinctive rich flavour that allowed Hungary to became one of the leading paprika producers in the world.
Kalocsa and Szeged in southern Hungary, boasting highest sunshine records, are at the heart of paprika production in Hungary. They compete against each other for the title of the Paprika Capital of Hungary.
The Hungarian Palfy brothers introduced semi-sweet paprika by removing the stalks and seeds from the pods.

In Hungarian villages at harvesting time the peppers are strung outside, all along the fences.
In Hungary paprika may be classified as delicate, sweet, noble, hot and smoked.
Spanish paprika (*pimentón*) is available in three versions – mild (*pimentón dulce*), moderately spicy (*pimentón agridulce*), and very spicy (*pimentón picante*).
Holland is a major production and distribution source of paprika, with much of it grown in greenhouses.
In Moroccan cuisine, paprika is usually augmented by a small amount of olive oil.

PARSLEY

The Holy Roman Emperor Charlemagne (c.742–814) munched through two cases a year of cheese flavoured with parsley seeds.
Ancient Greek gardens were often edged with parsley and rue.
The variety parsley root (or Hamburg parsley) is grown for its large root and has long been

Parsley leaves.

used as a winter vegetable in Germany, Holland, Austria, Hungary, Poland, and Russia.

Parsley root looks similar to a parsnip but tastes very different – rather like celeriac or a carrot that's been cooked with parsley, with hints of turnip and quite aromatic.

SAFFRON

Saffron has been used to dye royal garments and inspired the orange-gold colour of Buddhist priests' robes.

It has been used as an aphrodisiac, anaesthetic and to cure melancholy. In ancient Greece, crocus leaves were strewn on banqueting-hall floors, saffron water was sprinkled on theatre benches, and cushions were stuffed with saffron.

Saffron was once grown extensively round Saffron Walden, in Essex, England. One legend says that, during King Edward III's reign, a pilgrim returning to Walden from the Middle East hid a bulb of saffron in a hole in his stick. The bulb was planted and multiplied; soon saffron brought prosperity to the town that took its name. Saffron Hill in London is situated on a former saffron-growing estate (it was later picked by Charles

Saffron.

Dickens as the site of Fagin's Den in *Oliver Twist).*

In the thirteenth century Mediterranean pirates would often ignore shiploads of gold and instead steal saffron from Venetian and Genoan vessels.

Sesame seeds and pods.

SESAME

Sesame seeds – rich in calcium, zinc, magnesium, iron and trace elements – are especially helpful to women going through menopause.

Its name is derived from Arabic *simsim* and early Egyptian *semsent.*

During the Neolithic period, from about 7000 to about 4000 BCE, the fatty oils of olive and sesame were combined with fragrant plants to create ointments.

Sesame seeds were one of the first crops processed for oil as well as one of the earliest condiments.

In Hindu the word oil derives from the Sanskrit word for sesame.

In early Hindu legends sesame seeds represent immortality.

The world trades over a billion dollars' worth of sesame seeds each year.

For 4,000 years the seeds have been ground for flour and today still form the base for tahini, a delicious paste said to increase longevity.

500 sesame seeds equals 100 grams.

An Urdu saying describes a crowded place as 'not having room for even one sesame seed'.

King Darius of Persia gave young Alexander the Great (356–323 BCE) a sack of sesame seeds to show the number of men in his army; Alexander responded with a sack of mustard seeds to indicate both the number *and* fiery attitude of *his* army.

Tamarind. Facing page: Sunflower.

SUNFLOWER

The sunflower is sometimes also called Marigold of Peru, or *Chrysanthemum peruvianum*.

Its Latin name *Helianthus* derives from *helios* (sun) and *anthos* (flower).

Native Americans used them for food, bread, oil, ointments, dyes and body paints.

The protein-rich cake left after processing sunflowers to make oil is used to feed sheep, pigs, pigeons, rabbits – and poultry, for whom it is said to increase egg production.

TAMARIND

In Buddhist temples, tamarind fruit pulp is used to polish brass statues and lamps.

In south Indian homes it is used to clean the copper and bronze utensils.

The wood makes charcoal for gunpowder.

A decoction of the bark treats asthma.

It is an antiseptic and a laxative.

TURMERIC

Women in India did not use soap but instead used a turmeric germicidal cream treatment including chickpea flour or wheat husk mixed with milk. The wheat husk would remove dead cell tissue.

Turmeric soap is brilliant for curing acne.

Turmeric mixed with cauliflower may prevent prostate cancer.

It has a natural antivenom for king cobra snakebites.

Adding a spoonful of turmeric to the water in water-cooled radiators will help stop leaks.

INTERNATIONAL SPICES

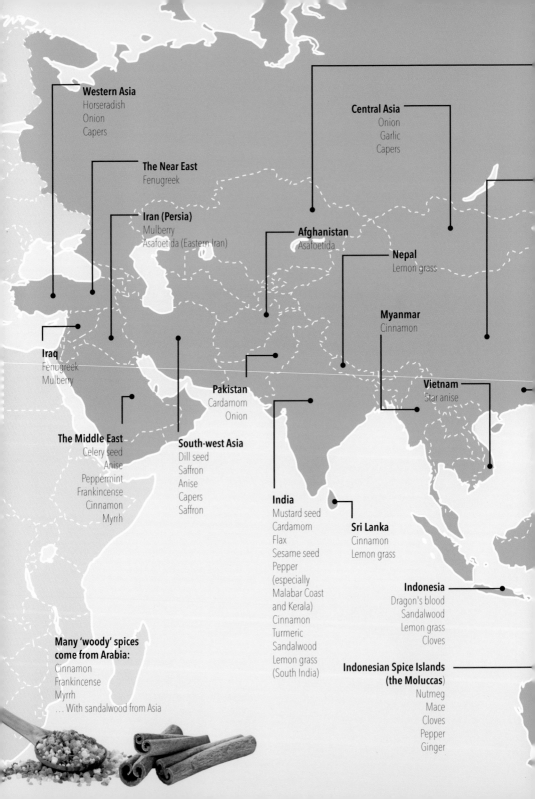

Western Asia
Horseradish
Onion
Capers

Central Asia
Onion
Garlic
Capers

The Near East
Fenugreek

Iran (Persia)
Mulberry
Asafoetida (Eastern Iran)

Afghanistan
Asafoetida

Nepal
Lemon grass

Myanmar
Cinnamon

Iraq
Fenugreek
Mulberry

Pakistan
Cardamom
Onion

Vietnam
Star anise

The Middle East
Celery seed
Anise
Peppermint
Frankincense
Cinnamon
Myrrh

South-west Asia
Dill seed
Saffron
Anise
Capers
Saffron

India
Mustard seed
Cardamom
Flax
Sesame seed
Pepper
(especially
Malabar Coast
and Kerala)
Cinnamon
Turmeric
Sandalwood
Lemon grass
(South India)

Sri Lanka
Cinnamon
Lemon grass

Indonesia
Dragon's blood
Sandalwood
Lemon grass
Cloves

**Many 'woody' spices
come from Arabia:**
Cinnamon
Frankincense
Myrrh
… With sandalwood from Asia

**Indonesian Spice Islands
(the Moluccas)**
Nutmeg
Mace
Cloves
Pepper
Ginger

All over Asia
Liquorice
Wormwood

China
Star anise
Mulberry
Cassia
Ginseng
Ginger
Flax
Rose petals
Star anise
Cassia
Rose hips

Hot spices include:
Turmeric (India)
Ginger (China)
Pepper (India)
Chilli and Paprika (Central and
   South America)

Tropical Asia
Makrut lime
Capers

Southeast Asia
Citrus zest
Makrut lime
Dragon's blood
Turmeric

**South Pacific near
(New Guinea)**
Coconut (possibly)
Allspice

**Australia and the
Southwest Pacific**
Citrus zest

SPICES FROM
ASIA
AND THE
PACIFIC

Sunflower is the state flower of Kansas and the national flower of Ukraine and of Russia.

USA, Canada
Sumac, Coconut

**West Indies
(St Vincent, Jamaica, Bermuda, Georgia)**
Arrowroot

Jamaica, Greater Antilles
Allspice

Guyana, Brazil
Arrowroot

Central America
Arrowroot (possibly)
Angelica
Chilli
Paprika (red pepper)
Allspice
Vanilla
Arrowroot
Angelica
Sunflower seeds

Mexico
Sunflower seeds
Allspice
Vanilla
Angelica
Chilli

South America
Chilli
Paprika (red pepper)
Coconut
Sunflower seeds (in Peru)

SPICES FROM THE
AMERICAS

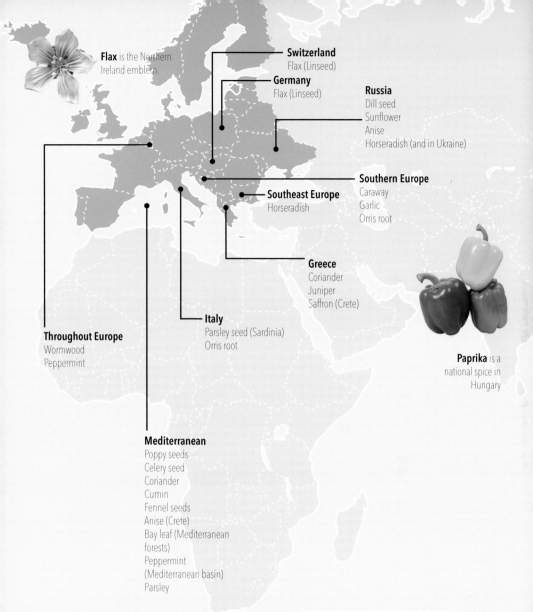

Flax is the Northern Ireland emblem.

Switzerland
Flax (Linseed)

Germany
Flax (Linseed)

Russia
Dill seed
Sunflower
Anise
Horseradish (and in Ukraine)

Southern Europe
Caraway
Garlic
Orris root

Southeast Europe
Horseradish

Greece
Coriander
Juniper
Saffron (Crete)

Italy
Parsley seed (Sardinia)
Orris root

Throughout Europe
Wormwood
Peppermint

Paprika is a national spice in Hungary

Mediterranean
Poppy seeds
Celery seed
Coriander
Cumin
Fennel seeds
Anise (Crete)
Bay leaf (Mediterranean forests)
Peppermint (Mediterranean basin)
Parsley

SPICES FROM
EUROPE

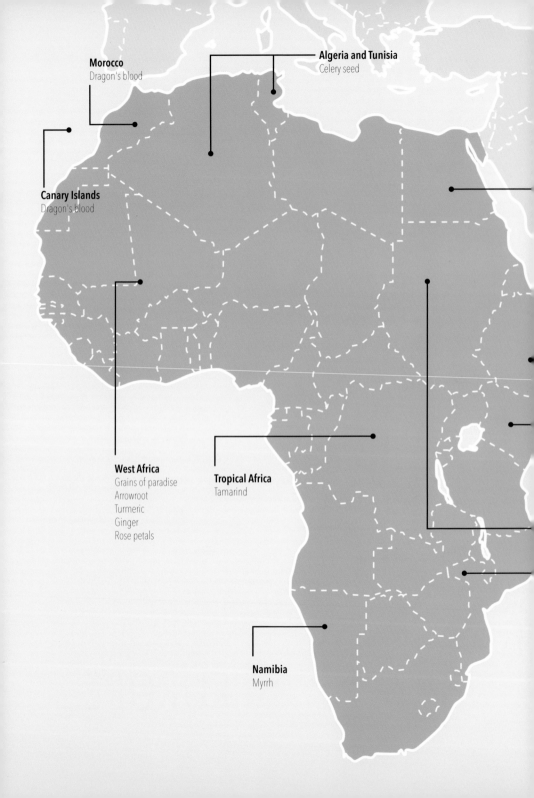

Morocco
Dragon's blood

Algeria and Tunisia
Celery seed

Canary Islands
Dragon's blood

West Africa
Grains of paradise
Arrowroot
Turmeric
Ginger
Rose petals

Tropical Africa
Tamarind

Namibia
Myrrh

SPICES FROM
AFRICA

Egypt
Fenugreek
Coriander
Cumin
Poppy seeds
Garlic

Ethiopia
Cinnamon
Myrrh

Somalia and Somaliland
Frankincense
Myrrh

All over Africa
Sumac
Liquorice

East Africa
Sesame seed
Myrhh

There are sweet spices, too:
Liquorice (Asia and Africa)
Peppermint (Europe, Middle East, Mediterranean)
Rose petals (China)
Vanilla (Mexico and Central America)
Angelica (Nordic origins, Syria or Africa)

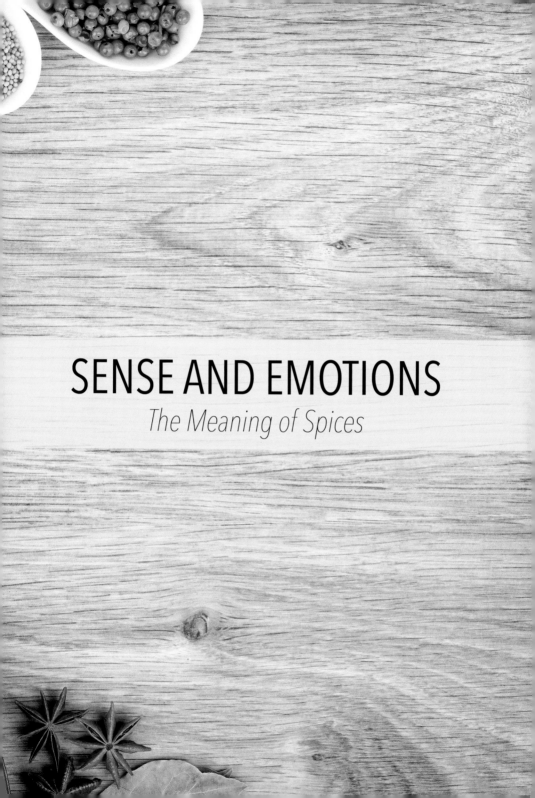

SENSE AND EMOTIONS
The Meaning of Spices

Allspice – good luck, healing, money, spiritual vibrations

Angelica – inspiration

Anise (aniseed) – restoration of youth

Bay leaf – consistency, glory, I change but in death

Caper – luck, lust, potency

Caraway – anti-theft, health, lust, mental powers, protection

Cardamon – paternal error

Celery seed – lust, mental powers, psychic powers

Chervil – sincerity

Chilli – fidelity, hex breaking, love

Cinnamon – love, luck, prosperity

Cloves – dignity, exorcism, love, money, protection

Coconut – chastity, protection, purification

Coriander – concealed merit, health and healing, hidden worth, love

Cumin – exorcism, fidelity, protection

Curry plant – protection

Dill seed – good spirits, luck, lust, money, protection

Dragon root – ardour

Dragon's blood – exorcism, love, potency, protection

Fennel – force, flattery, healing, protection, purification, strength

Fenugreek – money

Flax seed – beauty, healing, money, protection, psychic powers

Frankincense – exorcism, protection, spirituality

Garlic – courage, healing, deterring witches, vampires and theft, lust, protection

Ginger – love, money, power, success

Ginseng – beauty, healing, love, lust, protection, wishes

Facing page: Paprika and garlic strings.

Grains of paradise – love, luck, lust, money, wishes

Horseradish – exorcism, purification

Juniper berries – affection, anti-theft, exorcism, health, love, safety and protection

Lemongrass – protection against malice and gossip

Liquorice – fidelity, I declare against you, love, lust

Mace – psychic and mental powers

Mustard (black, brown, white) – expected meeting, fertility, indifference, mental powers, protection

Mulberry (black) – I will not survive you

Mulberry (white) – wisdom

Myrrh – exorcism, healing, gladness, protection, spirituality

Nutmeg – attraction, clairvoyance, prosperity

Onion – exorcism, healing, lust, money, prophetic dreams, protection

Orris root – divination, love, protection, purification, wisdom

Parsley seed – useful knowledge, festivity, joy, victory, woman of the house is boss

Pepper (green, black, red and white) – exorcism, protection

Peppermint – healing, love, psychic powers, purification, sleep

Rose petals – friendship, healing, love, , luck, passion, protection

Saffron – beware of excess; do not abuse our relationship

Saffron crocus – mirth

Sandalwood – exorcism, healing, meditation, protection, spirituality, tranquility

Savory – boldness, strong mental powers

Spearmint – warm sentiments

Sunflower seeds – adoration, fertility, health, wisdom, wishes

Sumac – intellectual excellence, splendid

Tarragon – lasting interest, long involvement

Turmeric – purification

Vanilla beans – affection, feminine attraction, love, lust, purity

Wormwood – calling spirits, love, protection psychic powers

Zest, lemon and citron – friendship, healing love, longevity, psychic powers, purification

Zest, orange – divination, love, luck, money

INDEX

Advieh 143
Allspice 90
Angelica 118
Anise (Aniseed) 46, 165
Aphrodisiac 10, 27, 48, 51, 57, 68, 79, 99, 101, 102, 113, 135, 166, 175
Apple pie spice 141
Arrowroot 104
Asafoetida 128

Bark 82, 85, 93
Bay leaf 130
Berries 52–79, 93
Bulbs 96–113

Cajun spices 143
Caper bush 122
Caraway 58
Cardamom 30, 164, 165
Cassia 84
Cayenne 56
Celery 166
Celery seed 22
Chilli 56
Chilli powder 142
Cilantro 26
Cinnamon 84, 164
Citrus zest 60
Cloves 136, 161, 164
Club moss 164
Coconut 64, 166–67
Coriander 26
Cumin 28, 164
Curry powder 142

Dill seed 20
Dragon's Blood 88

Fennel seed 32
Fenugreek 51
Five-spice powder (Chinese) 143
Flavours 159
Flax 36, 167–68
Flinders Rose 122
Frankincense 82
Fruits 52–79, 122

Garam masala 143
Garlic 98, 100, 164
Ginger 114
Ginseng 112
Goda masala 143
Grains of paradise 18, 164, 168

Hawaij 143
Honey 168–69
Horseradish 102

Iris 110

Juniper berries 70

Kaala masala 143
Kanda lasun masala 143
Khmeli suneli 143

Laurel 130
Leaves 118, 121, 122
Lemongrass 126
Lemon pepper 143
Liquorice 108
Linseed 36

Mace 38
Magic 89, 113, 125, 129,

135, 164
Makrut lime 62
Mitmita 143
Mixed (pudding) spice 141
Mixed spices 138–45
Montreal steak seasoning 143
Mulberry 72, 170
Mulling spices 141
Mustard 24, 170
Myrrh 86

Nutmeg 38, 161, 171

Onion 98
Orris root 110

Panch phoron 144
Paprika 54, 171–72
Parsley 172–73
Parsley seed 44
Pepper 74, 161
Peppermint 132, 136
Pickling spice 140
Poppy seeds 40
Poultry seasoning 144
Pumpkin pie spice (American) 141

Quatre épices 144

Ras el hanout 144
Red pepper 54
Resin 82, 86, 89, 129
Rhizomes 96–113
Roots 93–4, 96–113, 118, 122
Rose hips 134

Rose petals 134, 136

Saffron 124, 175
Salt 144, 146–53, 164, 165; Chinese 149; currency 150; routes 149–50; sayings 150; sources 148; towns 149
Sandalwood 94
Seeds 16–51, 118, 122
Sesame 48, 173, 178
Shichimi 144
Star anise 68
Sumac 92
Sunflower 34, 175
Superstition 58, 71, 101, 129, 164

Taco seasoning 144
Tamarind 76, 140, 175
Tandoori masala 144
Trees 82–95
Turmeric 106, 165, 175

Vadouvan 144

Vanilla beans 78

Witchcraft 58, 71, 101, 164
Wolf's claw 164
Worcestershire powder and sauce 140
Wormwood 120, 164, 165

Za'atar 144

IMAGE CREDITS

The author and publisher gratefully acknowledge the permission granted to reproduce the copyright material in this book. Every effort has been made to trace copyright holders and to obtain their permission for the use of illustrative material. The publisher apologizes for any errors or omissions in the credit list and would be grateful to be notified of any corrections that should be incorporated in future reprints or editions of this book.

Alamy 95. Corbis 74, 137. Digital Vision/Thinkstock/Sydney James 158. Gap Garden Photos 69. Dorling Kindersley/ Thinkstock 129. Hemera/Thinkstock: 33 Olga Tkachenko. 90 Tim Scott. 140 Jai Singh. Ingram Publishing/ Thinkstock 78. iStock/Thinkstock: 1 Kenishirotie. 2 Zheka-Boss. 5 Svetl. 6 tanjichica7. 8 peterzsuzsa. 9 Paul Grecaud. 10 NikiLitov. 11 marilyna. 12 klenova. 14 coffeechcolate. 17 locknloadlabrador. 20 seregam. 21 anna1311. 22 Alina Solovyova-Vincent. 23 anna1311. 24 bdspn; marilyna. 25 otme. 26 tycoon751. 28 dabjola. 29 Ezergil. 30 bdspn. 31 Lalith_Herath. 32 AndreyGorulko. 34 bksukkun. 35 HandmadePictures. 36 Frans Rombout. 37 Magone. 38 bdsn. 39 Lawrence Wee. 40 boonsom. 41 travellinglight. 42 YelenaYemchuk. 43 oksix. 44 ErikaMitchell. 45 Basya555. 46 semakokal. 47 Diana Taliun. 48 yogesh_more. 49 carroteater. 50 Watcha. 51 Watcha. 53 alfimimnill. 54 IceArnaudov. 55 Tuned_In. 56 KAdams66. 57 Ratana21. 58 Olesya Tseytlin. 59 sasimoto. 60 janaph. 61 egal. 62 ~User79fc5b7a_478; Ponpirun. 63 bangkaewphoto. 64 trex. 65 multik7. 66 serezniy; 467270582. 67 victoriya89. 68 Magone. 71 HandmadePictures. 72 msk.nina; lepas2004. 73 klazing. 75 Sensay. 76 jirkaejc. 77 mansum008. 79 Andreas Kraus. 80 ezza116. 82 marilyna. 83 zanskar. 84 AlexStar. 85 Helena Lovincic. 86 marilyn barbone, 87 Vladimir Melnik. 88 zanskar. 91 BravissimoS. 92 JackVandenHeuvel. 93 AndreyGorulko. 94 marilyna. 96 rakratchada. 98 Tamara Jovic. 99 bdspn; mkos83. 100 Buriy. 101 Nadalinna. 102 eldinledo. 103 Martina Chmielewski. 104 susansam. 106 GreenSeason. 107 Oliver Hoffmann. 108 sommail; eZeePics Studio. 109 dabjola. 110 Heike Rau. 112 KirsanovV. 13 koosen. 114 epantha. 116 fotokris. 118 marilyna. 119 MychkoAlezander. 120 sever180. 121 Marakit_Atinat. 122 serezni. 123 y. 123 JannHuizenga. 124 jonathan_steven. 125 george tsartsianidis. 126 Chris Leachman. 127 mansum008. 128 GeloKorol. 130 Andrelix. 131 sb-borg. 133 matka_Wariatka. 134 Sze Fei Wong. 135 Nadajda2015. 136 Magone. 139 ToniFlap. 140 zkruger. 141 tycoon751. 142 fotografiche. 145 matka_Wariatka. 146 tisskananat. 148 Mikhail Kokhanchikov. 151 NikiLitov. 153 Photoprofi30. 155 Elena Schweitzer. 157 svehlik. 161 Luis Santos. 163 Krzysztof Slusarczyk. 164 Elena_Ozornina. 165 marilyna; Toltek. 166 Diana Taliun; joannawnuk. 168 AlexStepanov. 169 Valengilda. 170 ChViroj; HandmadePictures; 171 silroby. 172 anna1311. 173 george tsartsianidis. 173 bdspn. 174 Amawasri. 175 mansum008. 177 Erdosain. 178 Alexlukin; marilyna. 179 maceofoto; Oliver Hoffmann; AndreyGorulko; bergamont. 180 Cobalt88. 181 Frans Rombout; Pratchaya. 183 sommail; matka_Wariatka; posterized; dianazh; cao chunhai. 184 karandaev. 186 Baloncici. 189 Ciungara. Photos.com/Thinkstock 11. Wavebreakmedia/Thinkstock/Wavebreakmedia Ltd 115.

AUTHOR'S NOTE

To avoid repetition and boring verbosity, such phrases as 'It is said that …' or 'People once used to believe …' have often been avoided in this text. But their omission in no way implies that such claims are beyond dispute, especially in the case of magic, witches, and miracle cures!

Any drug is dangerous if misused and some plant parts are poisonous or lethal. The author and publisher accept no responsibility for the contents and information in this book, neither can they endorse any of the medical 'traditions', many of which are either folklore or ancient and incomplete knowledge. They are included for interest's sake, not as a recommendation. Contradictions may apply if suffering from certain conditions, if pregnant, or if already taking prescribed medications so further research and advice should be sought from a qualified doctor before considering any spice remedies.

PRECAUTIONS

There is space here for only very brief descriptions of the medical uses of spices but many more details can be found in specialized books or websites that describe both present and ancient cures.

This book is an interesting glimpse into the importance of plant cures in historic times but neither the author nor the publishers can vouch for their efficacy or safe use. Indeed the old herbal 'Bibles' are full of precautionary advice.

ACKNOWLEDGEMENTS

Grateful thanks to all the Worth Press team for their amazing support.

BIBLIOGRAPHY

Baker, Margaret *Discovering the Folklore of Plants* Shire Publications (2011)

Bown, Deni *RHS Encyclopedia of Herbs and their Uses* Dorling Kindersley (1995)

Culpeper, Nicholas: *The British Herbal and Family Physician* Milner and Company (mid/late 1800s)

Czarra, Fred *Spices: A Global History* Reaktion Books (2012)

Day, Liz *Herb and Spice Guide: Fascinating Facts and Delicious Recipes* Schwartz (2009)

Divakaruni, Chitra *The Mistress Of Spices* Black Swan (1997)

Gambrelli, Fabienneb and Boussahba, Sophie *Spices: Volume 1: The History of Spices* and *Volume 2: The Flavor of Spices* Flammarion (2008)

Hemphill, Ian and Kate *The Spice and Herb Bible* Robert Rose Inc. (2014)

Langley, Andrew *The Little Book of Spice Tips* Absolute Press (2006)

Norman, Jill *The Complete Book of Spices* Dorling Kindersley (1990)

Botanical.com, *A Modern Herbal* by Mrs M Grieve